The Exceptional Child: Inclusion in Early Childhood Education

Join us on the web at

EarlyChildEd.delmar.cengage.com

The Exceptional Child: Inclusion in Early Childhood Education

Jennifer Johnson

Australia • Brazil • Japan • Korea • Mexico • Singapore • Spain • United Kingdom • United States

OUACHITA TECHNICAL COLLEGE

The Exceptional Child: Inclusion in Early Childhood Education

Jennifer Johnson

For product information and technology assistance, contact us at **Cengage Learning Customer & Sales Support, 1-800-354-9706**

For permission to use material from this text or product, submit all requests online at **www. cengage.com/ permissions.** Further permissions questions can be e-mailed to **permissionrequest@cengage.com.**

Library of Congress Control Number: 2007047756

ISBN-13: 978-1-4180-7404-3

ISBN-10: 1-4180-7404-7

Delmar
10 Davis Drive
Belmont, CA 94002-3098
USA

Cengage Learning is a leading provider of customized learning solutions with office locations around the globe, including Singapore, the United Kingdom, Australia, Mexico, Brazil, and Japan. Locate your local office at:
www.cengage.com/global

Cengage Learning products are represented in Canada by Nelson Education, Ltd.

To learn more about Delmar, visit
www.cengage.com/Delmar

Purchase any of our products at your local college store or at our preferred online store **www.ichapters.com**

Printed in the United States of America
2 3 4 5 6 7 8 12 11 10 09

TABLE OF CONTENTS

This tool was developed to help you, the budding teacher and/or child care provider, as you move into your first classroom.

INTRODUCTION

Throughout a college program of preparation to become an early childhood educator, students take many courses, read many textbooks. And their knowledge grows as they accumulate ideas from lectures, reading, experiences, and discussions. When they finish their coursework, graduate, and move into their first teaching positions, students often leave behind some of the books they have used. The hope is, however, that they will take with them the important ideas from their classes and books as they begin their own professional practice.

More experienced colleagues or mentors sometimes support teachers in their first teaching positions, helping them make the transition between college classroom and being responsible for a group of young children. Other times, new teachers are left to travel their own paths, relying on their own resources. Whatever your situation, this professional enhancement guide is designed to provide reminders of things you have learned, and resources to help you make sense of and apply what you learned during your college coursework.

Teachers of young children are under great pressure today. From families, there are the demands for support in their difficult task of childrearing in today's fast-paced and changing world. Some families become so overwhelmed with the tasks of parenting that they seem to leave too much responsibility on the shoulders of teachers and caregivers. From administrators and institutions, there are expectations that sometimes seem overwhelming. Teachers are being held accountable for children's learning in ways unprecedented in even the recent past. Public scrutiny has led to insistence on teaching practices that may seem contrary to the best interests of children or their teachers. New teachers may find themselves caught between the realities of the schools or centers where they find themselves, and their own philosophies and ideals of working with children. When faced with such dilemmas, it is important for these individuals to be able to fall back and reflect on what they know of best practices, renewing their professional determination to make appropriate decisions for children. This book provides some tools for that reflection.

These tools include:

- tips for getting off to a great start in your new environment

- information about typical and atypical developmental patterns of children from birth through age eight

- suggestions for materials that promote development for children from infancy through the primary grades

- tools to assist teachers in making observations on children and gathering data to help set appropriate goals for individual children

- guides for planning appropriate classroom experiences, including sample lesson plans

- a guide to introducing children to the joys of literacy

- a summary of the key ideas about Developmentally Appropriate Practice, the process of decision-making that allows teachers to provide optimum environments for children from birth through age eight

- professional development resources for teachers

- lists of other helpful resources

- case studies of relevant, realistic situations you may face, as well as best practices for successfully navigating through them

- insight into issues and trends facing early childhood educators today

Becoming a teacher is a process of continuing to grow, learn, reflect, and discover through experience. Having these resources may help you along your way. Good luck on your journey!

REFLECTIONS FOR GROWING TEACHERS

Teachers spend most of their time working with young children and their families. During the course of a day, questions and concerns arise, and decisions have to be made. Thus it is important that teachers become reflective about their work. Too often, teachers believe they are too busy to spend time thinking; however, experienced professional teachers learn that guided reflection sustains their best work. Growing teachers need to regularly take time to consider the questions and concerns that arise from their practice. Some teachers use journals to keep track of the process.

Use some of these questions to begin your reflection. Then add to them with questions from your own experience:

QUESTIONS FOR REFLECTION*

This day would have been better if . . .

_____

_____

I think I need to know more about . . .

_____

_____

One new thing I think I'll try this week is . . .

_____

_____

The highlight of this week was . . .

_____

_____

The observations this week made me think more about . . .

_____

_____

I think my favorite creative activity this year was . . .

_____

_____

One area where my teaching is changing is . . .

_____

_____

One area where my teaching needs to change is . . .

_____

_____

I just don't understand why . . .

_____

_____

I loved my job this week when . . .

_____

_____

I hated my job this week when . . .

_____

_____

One thing I can try to make better next week is . . .

_____

_____

The funniest thing I heard a child say this week was . . .

_____

_____

The family member I feel most comfortable with is . . .

_____

_____

And I think the reason for that is . . .

_____

_____

The family member I feel least comfortable with is . . .

_____

_____

And I think the reason for that is . . .

_____

_____

The biggest gains in learning have been made by . . .

_____

_____

And I think that this is because . . .

_____

_____

I'm working on a bad habit of . . .

_____

_____

Has my attitude about teaching changed this year? Why?

_____

_____

What have I done lately to spark the children's imagination and creativity?

_____

_____

One quote that I like to keep in mind is . . .

_____

_____

Dealing with _____

is the most difficult thing I had to face recently because . . .

_____

_____

My teaching style has been most influenced by . . .

_____

_____

In thinking more about children with exceptionalities in my curriculum, I believe . . .

_____

_____

If I were going to advise a brand-new teacher, the most helpful piece of advice would be . . .

_____

_____

I've been trying to facilitate friendships among the children by . . .

_____

_____

I really need to get started . . .

_____

_____

I used to . . .

_____

_____

but now I . . .

_____

_____

The child who has helped me learn the most is . . .

_____

_____

I learned . . .

_____

_____

I've grown in my communication by . . .

_____

_____

The best thing I've learned by observing is . . .

_____

_____

I still don't understand why . . .

_____

_____

One mistake I used to make that I don't make any longer is . . .

_____

_____

When I start the next year of teaching, one thing I will do more of is . . .

_____

_____

When I start the next year of teaching, one thing I won't do is . . .

_____

_____

One way I can help my children feel more competent is . . .

_____

_____

Something that I enjoy that I could share with the children in my class is . . .

_____

_____

When children have difficulty sharing, I . . .

_____

_____

*Adapted from ideas in Nilsen, *Week by Week*, 3E, 2004, Clifton Park, NY: Delmar.

TIPS FOR SUCCESS

Remember that you are a role model for the children. They are constantly watching how you dress, what you say and what you do.

BE A PROFESSIONAL

- Dress conservatively and follow your employer's clothing expectations. (You will probably be expected to wear closed-toe shoes to be safe and active with children; clothing should be clean, modest, and comfortable.)

- Be prepared and on time consistently.

- Avoid excessive absences.

- Always use appropriate language with children and adults.

- Be positive when talking to parents and show that you are forming a positive. relationship with their child. "Catch children doing something right," and share those accomplishments with parents. Challenges with children can be discussed after you have established trust with the parents.

BE A TEAM PLAYER

- Rely on team members to help you learn the parameters of your new position.

- Don't be afraid to ask questions of or for guidance from teammates.

- Show your support and be responsible.

- Step in to do your share of the work; don't expect others to clean up after you.

- Be of assistance to others whenever possible.

- Respect others' ideas and avoid telling them how to do things.

- Balance your ability to make decisions with following the lead of others.

- Never hesitate to double-check something with your teammates when you are in doubt.

LEARN ABOUT CHILDREN

- Be aware of their development physically, socially, emotionally, and cognitively.

- Assess children's development and plan curriculum that will enhance it

- Be aware that children will test you! (Children, especially of school age, will expect that you don't know the rules and may try to convince you to let them do things they previously have not been allowed to do.)

- Use positive management techniques with children.

MANAGEMENT TECHNIQUES FOR GAINING CHILDREN'S COOPERATION

There are myriad techniques that will help children cooperate; the following techniques are preventive in nature. Children need respectful reminders of expectations and adult support in performing to those expectations. Be sure that your expectations are age appropriate and individually appropriate.

- Use positive phrases and state exactly what you expect children to do. "Stand by the door" is more effective than "Don't go outside until everyone is ready."

- Avoid the words "no" and "don't." Be clear about what it is you want children to do, not what you don't want them to do.

- Sequence directions using "When-then." For example, "When things are put away where they belong, then we can go outside."

- Stay close. Merely standing near children can be enough to help manage behavior. Be aware, however, that if you are talking to another adult, children may act out because they are aware that they do not have your attention.

- Offer sufficient and appropriate choices. Children need a variety of activities that interest them and that will create opportunities for success.

GETTING STARTED

There is always a cadre of things to learn when starting a new position working with children. Use this fill-in-the blank section to customize this resource book to your specific environment.

What are the school's or center's hours of operation?

On school days: _____

_____

_____

On vacation days: _____

_____

_____

What is the basic daily schedule and what are my responsibilities during each of those time segments?

_____

_____

_____

_____

_____

_____

_____

What are the procedures for checking children in and out of the program?

_____

_____

_____

Do I call if I have to be absent? Who is my contact?

Name _____

Phone Number _____

What is the dress code for employees?

_____

_____

For what basic health and safety practices will I be responsible? Where are the materials stored for this? (Bleach, gloves, etc.)

Sanitizing tables _____

_____

_____

Cleaning and maintaining of equipment and materials: _____

_____

_____

_____

What are the emergency procedures?

Mildly injured child: _____

_____

_____

Earthquake/Tornado: _____

_____

_____

Fire: _____

_____

_____

First Aid: _____

_____

_____

Other: _____

_____

_____

DEVELOPMENTAL MILESTONES BY AGE FOR TYPICALLY DEVELOPING CHILDREN

Whether you are working with infants, toddlers, preschoolers, or primary-aged children, a teacher's first requirement is to have knowledge about how children develop and learn. In your college program, you no doubt studied child development. The following is an abbreviated version of the universal steps most children go through as they develop. Some children will move easily from one step to another, but other children move forward in one area but lag behind in others. Although not an exhaustive list, these milestones should be used as a guide for arranging an environment or planning activities in your room.

DEVELOPMENTAL CHECKLIST

Child's Name _____ Age _____

Observer _____ Date _____

BY SIX MONTHS:	Yes	No	Sometimes
Does the child...			
Show continued gains in height, weight, and head circumference?			
Reach for toys or objects when they are presented?			
Begin to roll from stomach to back?			
Sit with minimal support?			

BY SIX MONTHS:	Yes	No	Sometimes
Does the child...			
Transfer objects from one hand to the other?			
Raise up on arms, lifting head and chest, when placed on stomach?			
Babble, coo, and imitate sounds?			
Turn to locate the source of a sound?			
Focus on an object and follow its movement vertically and horizontally?			
Exhibit a blink reflex? Enjoy being held and cuddled?			
Recognize and respond to familiar faces?			
Begin sleeping six to eight hours through the night?			
Suck vigorously when it is time to eat?			
Enjoy (splash, coo) playing in water during bathtime?			

DEVELOPMENTAL ALERTS

Check with a health care provider or early childhood specialist if, by one month of age, the infant *does not*:

- Show alarm or "startle" responses to loud noise.

- Suck and swallow with ease.

- Show gains in height, weight, and head circumference.

- Grasp with equal strength with both hands.

- Make eye contact when awake and being held.

- Become quiet soon after being picked up.

- Roll head from side to side when placed on stomach.

- Express needs and emotions with cries and patterns of vocalizations that can be distinguished from one another.

- Stop crying when picked up and held.

DEVELOPMENTAL ALERTS

Check with a health care provider or early childhood specialist if, by four months of age, the infant *does not*:

- Continue to show steady increases in height, weight, and head circumference.
- Smile in response to the smiles of others (the social smile is a significant developmental milestone).
- Follow a moving object with eyes focusing together.
- Bring hands together over mid-chest.
- Turn head to locate sounds.
- Begin to raise head and upper body when placed on stomach.
- Reach for objects or familiar persons.

DEVELOPMENTAL CHECKLIST

Child's Name _____   Age _____

Observer _____   Date _____

BY TWELVE MONTHS:	Yes	No	Sometimes
Does the child...			
Walk with assistance?			
Roll a ball in imitation of an adult?			
Pick up objects with thumb and forefinger?			
Transfer objects from one hand to the other?			
Pick up dropped toys?			
Look directly at an adult's face?			
Imitate gestures: peek-a-boo, bye-bye, pat-a-cake?			
Find object hidden under a cup?			
Feed oneself crackers: munching, not sucking on them?			

BY TWELVE MONTHS:	Yes	No	Sometimes
Does the child . . .			
Hold cup with two hands; drink with assistance?			
Smile spontaneously?			
Turn head or come when name is called?			
Respond to "no"?			
Show hesitation with strangers; want to be picked up only by familiar persons?			
Respond differently to sounds: vacuum, phone, door?			
Look at a person who speaks to him or her?			
Respond to simple directions accompanied by gestures?			
Make several consonant-vowel combination sounds?			
Vocalize back to a person who has talked to him or her?			
Use intonation patterns that sound like scolding, asking, exclaiming?			
Say "da-da" or "ma-ma"?			

DEVELOPMENTAL ALERTS

Check with a health care provider or early *childhood specialist* if, by twelve months of age, the infant *does not*:

- Blink when fast-moving objects approach the eyes.
- Begin to cut teeth.
- Imitate simple sounds.
- Follow simple verbal requests: *come, bye-bye.*
- Pull self to a standing position.

DEVELOPMENTAL CHECKLIST

Child's Name _____ Age _____

Observer _____ Date _____

BY TWO YEARS:	Yes	No	Sometimes
Does the child...			
Walk alone?			
Bend over and pick up a toy without falling over?			
Seat oneself in child-size chair?			
Walk up and down stairs with assistance?			
Place several rings on a stick?			
Place five pegs in a pegboard?			
Turn pages two or three at a time?			
Scribble?			
Follow one-step direction involving something familiar: "Give me _____," "Show me _____," "Get a _____"?			
Match familiar objects?			
Use a spoon with some spilling?			
Drink from cup holding it with one hand unassisted?			
Chew food?			
Take off coat, shoe, sock?			
Zip and unzip large zipper?			
Name and point to oneself in a mirror?			
Refer to oneself by name?			
Imitate adult behavior in play—for example, feeds "baby"?			

BY TWO YEARS:	Yes	No	Sometimes
Does the child...			
Help put things away?			
Respond to specific words by showing what was named: toy, pet, family member?			
Ask for desired items (cookie) by name?			
Answer with name of object when asked, "What's that"?			
Make some two-word statements: "Daddy bye-bye"?			

DEVELOPMENTAL ALERTS

Check with a health care provider or early childhood specialist if, by twenty-four months of age, the child *does not*:

- Attempt to talk or repeat words.
- Understand some new words.
- Respond to simple questions with "yes" or "no."
- Walk alone (or with very little help).
- Exhibit a variety of emotions: anger, delight, fear.
- Show interest in pictures.
- Recognize self in mirror.
- Attempt self-feeding: hold own cup to mouth and drink.

DEVELOPMENTAL CHECKLIST

Child's Name _____   Age _____

Observer _____   Date _____

BY THREE YEARS:	Yes	No	Sometimes
Does the child...			
Run with coordination in a forward direction; avoid running into objects or people?			
Jump in place, two feet together?			

BY THREE YEARS:	Yes	No	Sometimes
Does the child...			
Walk on tiptoe?			
Throw ball (but without direction or aim)?			
Kick a ball forward?			
String four large beads?			
Turn pages in book singly?			
Hold crayon and imitate circular, vertical, horizontal strokes?			
Match shapes?			
Demonstrate number concepts of one and two: can select one or two and can tell if one or two objects.			
Use a spoon without spilling?			
Drink from a straw?			
Put on and take off coat?			
Wash and dry hands with some assistance?			
Watch other children, play near them, sometimes join in their play?			
Defend own possessions?			
Use objects in make believe play—for example, tin pan on head becomes helmet and crate becomes a spaceship?			
Respond to "Put _____ in the box" and "Take the _____ out of the box"?			
Select correct item on request: big versus little; one versus two?			
Identify objects by their use: show their own shoe when asked "What do you wear on your feet?"			
Ask questions?			
Tell about something with functional phrases that carry meaning: "Daddy go airplane" or "Me hungry now"?			

DEVELOPMENTAL ALERTS

Check with a health care provider or early childhood specialist if, by the third birthday, the child *does not*:

- Eat a fairly well-rounded diet, even though amounts are limited.
- Walk confidently with few stumbles or falls; climb steps with help.
- Avoid bumping into objects.
- Carry out simple, two-step directions: "Come to Daddy and bring your book"; express desires; ask questions.
- Point to and name familiar objects; use two- or three-word sentences.
- Enjoy being read to.
- Show interest in playing with other children: watching, perhaps imitating.
- Indicate a beginning interest in toilet training.
- Sort familiar objects according to a single characteristic such as type, color, or size.

DEVELOPMENTAL CHECKLIST

Child's Name _____   Age _____

Observer _____   Date _____

BY FOUR YEARS:	Yes	No	Sometimes
Does the child...			
Walk on a line?			
Balance on one foot briefly? Hop on one foot?			
Jump over an object six inches high and land on both feet together?			
Throw ball with direction?			
Copy circles and Xs?			
Match six colors?			
Count to five?			

BY FOUR YEARS:	Yes	No	Sometimes
Does the child . . .			
Pour well from a pitcher?			
Spread butter, jam with a knife?			
Button, unbutton large buttons?			
Know their own sex, age, last name?			
Use toilet independently and when needed?			
Wash and dry hands unassisted?			
Listen to stories for at least five minutes?			
Draw head of a person and at least one other body part?			
Play with other children?			
Share, take turns (with some assistance)?			
Engage in dramatic and pretend play?			
Respond appropriately to "Put it beside . . . " or "Put it under . . . "?			
Respond to two-step directions: "Give me the sweater and put the shoe on the floor"?			
Respond by selecting the correct object—for example, hard versus soft object?			
Answer "if," "what," and "when" questions?			
Answer questions about function: " What are books for?"?			

DEVELOPMENTAL ALERTS

Check with a health care provider or early childhood specialist if, by the fourth birthday, the child *does not*:

- Have intelligible speech most of the time (if there is cause for concern, have children's hearing checked).

- Understand and follow simple commands and directions.

- State own name and age.

- Enjoy playing near or with other children.
- Use three- to four-word sentences.
- Ask questions.
- Stay with an activity for three or four minutes; play alone several minutes at a time.
- Jump in place without falling.
- Balance on one foot, at least briefly.
- Help with dressing self.

DEVELOPMENTAL CHECKLIST

Child's Name _____   Age _____

Observer _____   Date _____

BY FIVE YEARS:	Yes	No	Sometimes
Does the child...			
Walk backward, heel to toe?			
Walk up and down stairs, alternating feet?			
Cut on line with scissors?			
Print some letters?			
Point to and name three shapes?			
Group common related objects: shoe, sock, and foot: apple, orange, and plum?			
Demonstrate number concepts to four or five?			
Cut food with a knife: celery, sandwich?			
Lace shoes?			
Read from story picture book (tell story by looking at pictures)?			
Draw a person with three to six body parts?			
Play and interact with other children; engage in dramatic play that is close to reality?			

BY FIVE YEARS:	Yes	No	Sometimes
Does the child...			
Build complex structures with blocks or other building materials?			
Respond to simple three-step directions: "Give me the pencil, put the book on the table, and hold the comb in your hand"?			
Respond correctly when asked to show penny, nickel, and dime?			
Ask "How" questions?			
Respond verbally to "Hi" and "How are you"?			
Tell about event using past and future tenses?			
Use conjunctions to string words and phrases together—for example, "I saw a bear and a zebra and a giraffe at the zoo"?			

DEVELOPMENTAL ALERTS

Check with a health care provider or early childhood specialist if, by the fifth birthday, the child *does not*:

- State own name in full.

- Recognize simple shapes: circle, square, triangle.

- Catch a large ball when bounced (if there is any cause for concern, have child's vision checked).

- Speak so as to be understood by strangers (if there is any cause for concern, have child's hearing checked).

- Have good control of posture and movement.

- Hop on one foot.

- Appear interested in, and responsive to, surroundings.

- Respond to statements without constantly asking to have them repeated.

- Dress self with minimal adult assistance; manage buttons, zippers.

- Take care of own toilet needs; have good bowel and bladder control with infrequent accidents.

DEVELOPMENTAL CHECKLIST

Child's Name _____   Age _____

Observer _____   Date _____

BY SIX YEARS:	Yes	No	Sometimes
Does the child . . .			
Walk across a balance beam?			
Skip with alternating feet?			
Hop for several seconds on one foot?			
Cut out simple shapes?			
Copy own first name?			
Show well-established handedness; demonstrate consistent right- or left-handedness?			
Sort objects on one or more dimensions: color, shape, or function?			
Name most letters and numerals?			
Count by rote to 10: know what number comes next?			
Dress self completely, tie bows?			
Brush teeth unassisted?			
Have some concept of clock time in relation to daily schedule?			
Cross street safely?			
Draw a person with head, trunk, legs, arms, and features; often add clothing details?			
Play simple board games?			
Engage in cooperative play with other children, involving group decisions, role assignments, rule observance?			
Use construction toys, such as Legos, blocks, to make recognizable structures?			
Do fifteen-piece puzzles?			

BY SIX YEARS:	Yes	No	Sometimes
Does the child...			
Use all grammatical structures: pronouns, plurals, verb tenses, conjunctions?			
Use complex sentences; carry on conversations?			

DEVELOPMENTAL ALERTS

Check with a health care provider or early childhood specialist if, by the sixth birthday, the child *does not*:

■ Alternate feet when walking up and down stairs.

■ Speak in a moderate voice: neither too loud, too soft, too high, too low.

■ Follow simple directions in stated order: "Please go to the cupboard, get a cup, and bring it to me."

■ Use four to five words in acceptable sentence structure.

■ Cut on a line with scissors.

■ Sit still and listen to an entire short story (five to seven minutes).

■ Maintain eye contact when spoken to (unless this is a cultural taboo).

■ Play well with other children.

■ Perform most self-grooming tasks independently: brush teeth, wash hands and face.

DEVELOPMENTAL CHECKLIST

Child's Name _____   Age _____

Observer _____   Date _____

BY SEVEN YEARS:	Yes	No	Sometimes
Does the child...			
Concentrate on completing puzzles and board games?			
Ask many questions?			
Use correct verb tenses, word order, and sentence structure in conversation?			

BY SEVEN YEARS:	Yes	No	Sometimes
Does the child . . .			
Correctly identify right and left hands?			
Make friends easily?			
Show some control of anger, using words instead of physical aggression?			
Participate in play that requires teamwork and rule observance?			
Seek adult approval for efforts?			
Enjoy reading and being read to?			
Use pencil to write words and numbers?			
Sleep undisturbed through the night?			
Catch a tennis ball, walk across balance beam, hit ball with bat?			
Plan and carry out simple projects with minimal adult help?			
Tie own shoes?			
Draw pictures with greater detail and sense of proportion?			
Care for own personal needs with some adult supervision? Wash hands? Brush teeth? Use the toilet? Dress self?			
Show some understanding of cause-and-effect concepts?			

DEVELOPMENTAL ALERTS

Check with a health care provider or early childhood specialist if, by the seventh birthday, the child *does not*:

- Show some interest in reading and trying to reproduce letters, especially own name.
- Show signs of ongoing growth: increasing height and weight; continuing motor development such as running, jumping, balancing.

- Follow simple, multiple-step directions: "Finish your book, put it on the shelf, and then put on your coat."

- Follow through with instructions and complete simple tasks: putting dishes in the sink, picking up clothes, finishing a puzzle. *Note*: All children forget. Task incompletion is not a problem unless a child *repeatedly* leaves tasks unfinished.

- Begin to develop alternatives to excessive use of inappropriate behaviors in order to get own way.

- Develop a steady decrease in tension-type behaviors that may have developed with starting school: repeated grimacing or facial tics; eye twitching, grinding of teeth, regressive soiling or wetting, frequent stomachaches, refusing to go to school.

DEVELOPMENTAL CHECKLIST

Child's Name _____   Age _____

Observer _____   Date _____

BY EIGHT AND NINE YEARS:	Yes	No	Sometimes
Does the child...			
Have energy to play, continuing growth, few illnesses?			
Use pencil in a deliberate and controlled manner?			
Express relatively complex thoughts in a clear and logical fashion?			
Carry out multiple four- to five-step instructions?			
Become less easily frustrated with own performance?			
Interact and play cooperatively with other children?			
Show interest in creative expression: telling stories, jokes, writing, drawing, singing?			
Use eating utensils with ease?			
Have a good appetite? Show interest in trying new foods?			

BY EIGHT AND NINE YEARS:	Yes	No	Sometimes
Does the child...			
Know how to tell time?			
Have control of bowel and bladder functions?			
Participate in some group activities: games, sports, plays?			
Want to go to school? Seem disappointed if must miss a day?			
Demonstrate beginning skills in reading, writing, and math?			
Accept responsibility and complete work independently?			
Handle stressful situations without becoming overly upset?			

DEVELOPMENTAL ALERTS

Check with a health care provider or early childhood specialist if, by the eighth birthday, the child *does not*:

- Attend to the task at hand: show longer periods of sitting quietly, listening, responding appropriately.

- Follow through on simple instructions.

- Go to school willingly most days (of concern are excessive complaints about stomachaches or headaches when getting ready for school).

- Make friends (observe closely to see if the child plays alone most of the time or withdraws consistently from contact with other children).

- Sleep soundly most nights (frequent and recurring nightmares or bad dreams are usually at a minimum at this age).

- Seem to see or hear adequately at times (of concern are squinting, rubbing eyes excessively, asking frequently to have things repeated).

- Handle stressful situations without undue emotional upset (excessive crying, sleeping or eating disturbances, withdrawal, frequent anxiety).

- Assume responsibility for personal care (dressing, bathing, feeding self) most of the time.

- Show improved motor skills.

DEVELOPMENTAL ALERTS

Check with a health care provider or early childhood specialist if, by the ninth birthday, the child *does not*:

- Exhibit a good appetite and continued weight gain (some children, especially girls, may already begin to show early signs of an eating disorder).

- Experience fewer illnesses.

- Show improved motor skills in terms of agility, speed, and balance.

- Understand abstract concepts and use complex thought processes to problem-solve.

- Enjoy school and the challenge of learning.

- Follow through on multiple-step instructions.

- Express ideas clearly and fluently.

- Form friendships with other children and enjoy participating in group activities.

As with the list of milestones by age, this list is not exhaustive, but it can be used to arrange an environment or to plan activities in your room.

BIRTH TO 8 YEARS**

Cognitive	Date Observed
Recognizes familiar objects and people at a distance	
Exhibits hand-eye coordination	
Finds partially hidden objects	
Explores objects in many different ways (shaking, banging, throwing, dropping)	
Finds hidden objects easily	
Imitates gestures	
Begins make-believe play	
Plays make-believe with dolls, animals, and people	
Recalls parts of a story	
Engages in fantasy play	
Language	
Smiles at the sound of voice	
Cooing noises; vocal play	
Distinguishes emotions by tone of voice	

Cognitive	Date Observed
Responds to sound by making sounds	
Uses voice to express joy and displeasure	
Syllable repetition begins	
Makes simple gestures such as shaking head for "no"	
Babbles with inflection	
Uses exclamations such as "oh-oh"	
Tells stories	
Social/Emotional	
Begins to develop a social smile	
Enjoys playing with other people and may cry when playing stops	
Becomes more communicative and expressive with face and body	
Imitates some movements and facial expressions	
Enjoys social play	
Interested in mirror images	
Responds to other people's expression of emotion	
Enjoys imitating people in his play	
Repeats sounds or gestures for attention	
Expresses a wide range of emotions	
More inventive in fantasy play	
May have imaginary friends or see monsters	
Wants to please and be with friends	
More likely to agree to rules	
Likes to sing, dance, and act	
Physical	
Transfers objects from hand to hand	
Looks for toy beyond tracking range	
Tracks moving objects with ease	
Grasps objects dangling in front of him	

Physical	
Looks for fallen toys	
Uses pincer grasp (grasp using thumb and index finger)	
Bangs two one-inch cubes together	
Puts objects into container	
Takes objects out of container	
Pokes with index finger	
Tries to imitate scribbling	
Scribbles spontaneously	
Makes vertical, horizontal, circular strokes with pencil or crayon	
Copies square shapes	
Draws a person with 2-4 body parts	
Uses scissors	
Draws circles and squares	
Begins to copy some capital letters	
Copies triangle and other geometric patterns	
Draws person with body	
Prints some letters	

** Content in this section adapted from Allen, E.A. and Marotz, L., *Developmental Profiles: Pre-birth through Twelve*, 5th edition, published by Delmar, a part of Cengage Learning.

MATERIALS FOR ALL CHILDREN

Children construct their own understanding of the world around them as they interact with appropriate materials and with other people. Teachers play an important role in providing choices of good quality playthings that match children's developmental abilities and interests. When budgets are limited, it is vital that teachers be able to select toys and materials that will provide optimum learning opportunities. Creative teachers learn how to find toys in all places, and to make playthings out of recycled materials.

Criteria for Selecting Play Equipment for Young Children

1. A young child's playthings should be as free of detail as possible.

   A child needs freedom to express himself by creating his own childlike world; too much detail hampers him. Blocks are the best example of "unstructured" toys. Blocks, construction sets, and other unstructured toys and equipment such as clay, sand, and paints allow the imagination free rein and are basic playthings.

2. A good plaything should stimulate children to do things for themselves.

   Equipment that makes the child a spectator, such as a mechanical duck, may entertain for the moment but has little or no play value. The equipment provided for play should encourage children to explore and create or should offer the opportunity for dramatic play.

3. Young children need large, easily manipulated playthings.
   Toys too small can be a source of frustration because the child's muscular coordination is not yet developed enough to handle the smaller forms and shapes. A child's muscles develop through play. A child needs equipment for climbing and balancing.

4. The material from which a plaything is made has an important role in the play of children.
   Warmth and pleasurable touch are significant, and the most satisfactory materials are wood and cloth.

5. The durability of the plaything is of utmost importance.
   Play materials must be sturdy. Axles and wheels must be strong to support a child's weight.

6. The toy must "work."
   Children become frustrated when a door or drawer won't shut, wheels get stuck, or figures won't stand up. Parts should move correctly and maintenance should be easy.

7. The construction of a plaything should be simple enough for a child to comprehend.
   The mechanics should be visible and easily grasped.

8. A plaything should encourage cooperative play.
   As we seek to teach children to work and play together, we should supply the environment that stimulates such play.

9. The total usefulness of the plaything must be considered in comparing price.
   Will it last several children through several stages of their playing lives? What are some good toys and play materials for young children? All ages are approximate. Most suggestions for younger children are also appropriate for older children.

The lists that follow suggest the materials that are priorities for children at particular levels of development.

FOR YOUNG INFANTS (BIRTH THROUGH SIX MONTHS)

- unbreakable mirrors that can be attached low on walls or near changing tables and cribs

- washable stuffed toys or rag dolls with stitched faces and eyes

- mobiles and visuals hung out of reach

- grasping toys such as simple rattles, squeeze toys, keys on ring, clutch or texture balls

- hanging toys for batting

- wrist or ankle bells

FOR OLDER, MOBILE INFANTS (SEVEN THROUGH TWELVE MONTHS)

- soft rubber animals for grasping
- simple one piece vehicles six to eight inches and with large wheels
- grasping toys for skill development: toys on suction cups, stacking rings, nesting cups, squeeze toys, plastic pop beads, bean bags, busy boxes
- containers and objects to fill and dump
- small cloth, plastic, and board books
- soft cloth or foam blocks for stacking
- simple floating objects for water play
- balls of all kinds, including some with special effects
- low soft climbing platforms
- large unbreakable mirrors
- infant swings for outdoors
- recorded music and songs

FOR TODDLERS (ONE THROUGH THREE YEARS)

For fine motor skills, toddlers need:

- nesting materials
- sand and water play toys such as funnels, colanders, small sand tools
- simple activity boxes, with doors, lids, switches, more complex after about 18 months: turning knob or key
- pegboards with large pegs
- four to five piece stacking materials
- pop beads and stringing beads
- simple three to five piece puzzles, with knobs, familiar shapes
- simple matching materials
- books, including tactile books: cloth, plastic, and board picture books

For gross motor skills, toddlers need:

- push and pull toys
- simple doll carriages and wagons
- stable riding toys with four wheels and no pedals
- balls of all sizes
- tunnels for crawling through
- tumbling mats and low climbing platforms

For pretend play, toddlers need:

- small wood or plastic people and animal figures
- small cars and trucks
- dolls
- plastic dishes and pots and pans
- doll beds
- hats
- simple dressups
- telephones
- scarves and fabrics

For sensory play, toddlers need:

- recorded music and player
- play dough
- finger paint
- large nontoxic crayons
- sturdy paper
- simple musical instruments

FOR CHILDREN AGES THREE THROUGH FIVE

For gross motor play, children need:

- small wagons and wheelbarrows
- replications of adult tools for pushing and pretend play such as a lawn mower or shopping cart

- scooters

- tricycles and other vehicles with steering ability

- riding toys for more than one child

- balls of all sizes, especially 10-12 inch balls for kicking and throwing

- hollow plastic bat and lightweight ball

- jump rope

- stationary outdoor climbing equipment

- slides and ladders

- outdoor building materials, tires, and other loose parts

Exploration and mastery play materials:

- sand and water play materials: measures, funnels, tubes, sand tools

- construction materials: unit blocks, large hollow blocks

- lego-type plastic interlocking blocks

- puzzles, including fit-in puzzles and large, simple jigsaw puzzles with varying numbers of pieces, according to children's age

- pattern-making materials, such as beads for stringing, pegboards, mosaic boards, felt boards, and color cubes

- dressing, lacing, and stringing materials: sewing cards and dressing frames

- collections of small plastic objects, for matching, sorting, and ordering, by color, shape, size, or other category concepts

- simple, concrete number materials for counting and matching to numerals

- measuring materials: scales, measuring cups for liquids

- science materials: magnifying glass, color paddles, and objects from the natural world, including pets

- beginning computer programs

- games that use concepts such as color or counting: dominoes, lotto games, bingo by color, number, or picture, first board games, and Memory™

- books of all kinds, including picture books, realistic stories, alphabet picture books, poetry, and information books

- writing center materials: clipboards, colored pencils, old calendars, envelopes, notepads, stationary, rubber stamps and ink pads, rulers, magnetic letters, stencil shapes, stickers, file cards, and office materials.

For pretend play, children need:

- dolls of various ethnic and gender appearance, with clothes and other accessories
- housekeeping equipment
- variety of dressups, including those related to various roles and themes
- transportation toys
- hand puppets
- animal and human figures for play scenes
- full length, unbreakable mirror

For creative play, children need:

- art and craft materials, including: crayons, markers, easel, paintbrushes, paint and finger paint, varieties of paper, chalkboard and chalk, safety scissors, glue, collage materials, clay and playdough, and tools to use with them
- workbench with hammer, saw, and nails
- musical instruments
- recorded music for singing, movement and dancing, listening, and for using with rhythm instruments

FOR CHILDREN SIX THROUGH EIGHT YEARS***

For gross motor play, children need:

- balls and sports equipment for beginning team play, such as soccer, baseball
- complex climbing structures: ropes, ladders, rings, and hanging bars
- materials for target practice
- mats for acrobatics
- bicycles and scooters

For exploration and mastery play, children need:

- construction materials for large constructions and for creating models: metal parts, nuts and bolts

- puzzles, including 100-piece jigsaw puzzles and three-dimensional puzzles like Rubik's Cubes

- craft materials for braiding, weaving, knitting, leather craft, jewelry making, and sewing

- pattern-making materials: mosaic tiles and geometric puzzles

- games: word games, simple card games, reading and spelling games, number and counting games, beginning strategy games such as checkers.

- materials for specific learning: printing materials, math manipulatives, measuring materials, science materials, and computer programs for language arts, number and concept development, and for problem-solving activities

- books at a variety of levels for beginning readers (see list that follows this section).

For creative activities, children need:

- a variety of markers, colored pencils, chalks, paintbrushes and paints, art paper for tracing and drawing

- clay and tools, including pottery wheel

- workbench with wood and a variety of tools

- musical instruments such as guitars and recorders

- music for singing and movement

- audiovisual materials for independent use

RECYCLED MATERIALS

Remember that recycled materials have many uses for exploration and creativity. The following materials can be valuable instructional tools in the art program as well as in other curriculum areas:

1. Empty plastic containers: detergent bottles, bleach bottles, old plastic containers. These can be used for constructing scoops, storing art materials, etc.

2. Buttons: all colors and sizes. These are excellent for collages, assemblages, as well as sorting, counting, matching, etc.

3. Egg shells. These can be washed, dried, and colored with food coloring for art projects.

4. Coffee or shortening cans and lids. These can be covered with adhesive paper and used for the storage of art supplies, games, and manipulatives materials.

5. Magazines with colorful pictures. These are excellent for making collages, murals, and posters.

6. Scraps of fabric: felt, silk, cotton, oil cloth, etc. These can be used to make "fabric boards" with the name of each fabric written under a small swatch attached to the board, as well as for collages, puppets, etc.

7. Yarn scraps. These can be used for separating buttons into sets and for art activities.

8. Styrofoam scraps.

9. Scraps of lace, rick rack, or decorative trim.

10. Bottles with sprinkler tops. Excellent for water play and for mixing water and finger paint.

11. Wallpaper books of discontinued patterns.

12. Paper doilies.

13. Discarded wrapping paper.

14. Paint color cards from paint/hardware stores.

15. Old paintbrushes.

16. Old jewelry and beads.

17. Old muffin tins. These are effective for sorting small objects and mixing paint.

18. Tongue depressors or ice cream sticks. These make good counters for math and are good for art construction projects, stick puppets, etc.

19. Wooden clothespins. These are good for making "people," for construction projects, for hanging up paintings to dry.

***Some ideas adapted from *The Right Stuff for Children Birth to 8: Selecting play materials to support development.* M. Bronson. Washington, D.C.: NAEYC, 1995.

1

OBSERVATION

BEGINNING THE SKILL OF OBSERVATION

There are a variety of assessment tools that can be used to guage children's development. Using these assessment tools in conjunction with developmental milestones helps caregivers recognize a child's developmental accomplishments as well as determine the child's next growth steps. The teacher needs to observe each child to determine the level to which each child is performing independently so that instruction can begin. This knowledge is useful in planning curriculum, in designing the room environment for success, and in establishing appropriate behavior management techniques that help children manage their own behavior. No doubt your college practicum experience taught you the logistics of observing: using objective description and recording specific, dated, brief, and factual information. Observation can take many forms; the most common include:

- anecdotal records

- running records

- checklists

- time or event sampling

ANECDOTAL RECORDS

Anecdotal records are brief notes taken by the teacher while the child is performing a task. At first this may seem daunting, but it will become part of your daily routine. Keep a small spiral notebook and pen or pencil in your pocket. When a child begins an activity, watch what the child does and write down three to four things that you observe the child doing. Remember to note only the facts. For example:

> Jing Mae picked up magnifying glass, looked at flower-picked up paper, went to easel, and began to draw a flower.

As time permits, probably during nap time, the brief notes are turned into a full scenario so that anyone could read the record at a later date:

ANECDOTAL RECORD				
Child's Name: Jing Mae			Age: 3 yr. 5 mo	
Observer's Name: Jorge			Date: April 27, 2007	
What actually happened/What I saw	**Developmental Interpretation** (Select one or two of the following)			
Jing Mae picked up the magnifying glass set out for the children to pick up as they chose and looked closely at the flower. Brought the flower to her teacher who shared in the observation. A conversation took place. Jing Mae then went to the art area and drew a picture of a flower.	Interest in learning		Self esteem/self concept	x
	Cultural acceptance		Problem solving	
	Interest in real life mathematical concepts		Interactions with adults	x
	Literacy		Interactions with peers	
	Language expression/ comprehension		Self regulation	
	Safe/healthy behavior		Self-help skills	
	Gross motor skills		Fine motor skills	x

ANECDOTAL RECORD

Child's Name: _____   Date:

Observer's Name: _____

What actually happened/What I saw	Developmental Interpretation (Select one or two of the following)			
	Interest in learning		Self esteem/self concept	
	Cultural acceptance		Problem solving	
	Interest in real life mathematical concepts		Interactions with adults	
	Literacy		Interactions with peers	
	Language expression/ comprehension		Self regulation	
	Safe/healthy behavior		Self-help skills	
	Gross motor skills		Fine motor skills	

RUNNING RECORD

Another form of authentic assessment is the running record. It covers a longer span of time and gives significantly more information than an anecdotal record. A running record will give you information about other developmental areas because of its very detailed nature. This form of observation requires the caregiver not to be involved with children for several minutes while writing the observation. You will be setting yourself apart from the children and writing continuously, in as much detail as possible. You will write what the child does and says, by herself and in interactions with other people and materials. Use phrases that are objective as previously described. Avoid interpretative and judgmental language while writing. Note that the format for this form of assessment is two columns. The left column is for writing the actual observations and the right column is for connecting the observations to aspects of development. Remember to date all observations so you can notice developmental change over time. Note also that running records often have a specific developmental focus such as "social interactions."

RUNNING RECORD

Child's Name: Meaghan   Age: 4 yr. 5 mo

Observer's Name: Susan   Date: April 27, 2007

Developmental Focus: Social interactions with peers

Meaghan and Luke were playing in the water table. The teacher had left out objects and a chart for the children to predict which objects would sink and float. After making their predictions, the children began the experiment. Meaghan told Luke, "I am right, you are wrong. The cotton ball will float." Luke said, "Let's try it and see." The cotton ball was placed in the water. At first it floated, but after a few seconds, the cotton ball sank. The teacher came over to see how things were going and questioned Luke as to why the cotton ball sank. He said, "because the cotton ball drank the water." Meaghan was not happy about being wrong, but conceded for now. The two moved on to the next object and their prediction.	Participates in cooperative activities Early literacy/expressive language Expresses empathy Communicates knowledge of growing skills Self regulation/controls emotions Stands up for own rights Asks for what she needs Gross motor skills Math skill Self awareness

CHECKLIST

A checklist is often used as a means of assessment because it is one of the easiest assessment tools to use. A checklist consists of a predetermined list of developmental criteria for which the observer indicates "yes" or "no." The observer reads the developmental criteria and makes a checkmark if the decision is a "yes." The criteria should be clearly observable. This form of assessment requires that additional notes be recorded. Many teachers design their own checklists to fit the specific needs of their program. The following checklist is an example of one that might be used to assess social skills of children:

SOCIAL SKILLS CHECKLIST

Child's name: _____   Age: ___ yr. __ mo. __

Observer's Name: _____

Skills	Dates
❏ Desires and can work near other children	
❏ Interacts witha other children	
❏ Takes turns with other children	
❏ Enters play with others in positive manner	
❏ Shares materials and supplies	
❏ Stands up for own rights in positive manner	
❏ Forms friendships with peers	
❏ Engages in positive commentary on other children's work	
❏ Shows empathy	
❏ Negotiates compromises with other children	
❏ Demonstrates prosocial behavior	
❏ Participates in cooperative group activities	
❏ Resolves conflicts with adult prompts	
❏ Resolves conflicts without adult prompts	

Make checklists for each center in your classroom and hang them on clipboards. When you observe the children at play in each center, check off skills by placing a date in the appropriate box.

TIME OR EVENT SAMPLING

The last type of observation that a teacher should perform is a time or event sampling. These are similar in focus, but different, too. A **time sampling** asks the teacher to set a timer, and each time the timer goes off, the teacher looks at a particular child and writes down what the child is doing. Again only the facts are written, nothing else:

> The timer is set to go off every ten minutes. I will look at Johnny and see what he is doing when I hear the timer. The timer goes off, I look at Johnny. He is sorting the objects by color.
>
> The timer goes off again, he now has three piles.

As mentioned, an **event sampling** is similar; however, the teacher looks at events instead of being directed by a timer. The teacher zeros in on an event and writes down all that she sees pertaining to the event.

> Johnny is sorting shapes. He does not talk while doing his work. He chooses to sort by color. The teacher is watching to see what he will do with the two shapes that have more than one color. Johnny puts those back in the box.

Assessment and observation may seem overwhelming as you begin your career in Early Childhood. Do not shy away from it. Take the challenge and begin to look for the positive aspects of learning and mastering a new skill. Picture yourself as a student in your classroom and imagine what it is like to perfect something your teacher has just asked you to do. How does it make you feel? Now begin.

2

CHILDREN WITH EXCEPTIONALITIES AND THE LAW

LATEST UPDATES ON IDEA

The 2004 Individuals with Disabilities Education Improvement Act (IDEIA), PL 108-446, amended and updated the original Individuals with Disabilities Education Act (IDEA) of 1997. The new law, commonly known as IDEA 2004, went into effect on July 1, 2005. The revision maintains the integrity of IDEA with a few significant modifications:

- Extensive definition of "highly qualified" special education teachers—the new definition requires special education teachers to hold at least a B.A., and to obtain full state special education licensure or equivalent; there is no provision for a temporary or emergency licensure.

- Extensive provisions aimed at ensuring special education and related services for children with disabilities who are homeless or otherwise members of highly mobile populations—the provision requires the school to appoint a surrogate within 30 days of the request to place so that there is not a lapse in services for the child.

- Significant changes to procedural safeguards, including:
  - The addition of a resolution session prior to a due process hearing to encourage the parties to resolve their dispute—within 15 days of the parent's complaint, the **Local Education Agency** (LEA) calls a meeting with the parent, school personnel, and LEA to try to resolve the issue. If it is resolved, a legally binding agreement is signed and upheld in District Courts; if not, the parent can pursue the hearing within 30 days of the original complaint.

- Functional behavioral assessment—when a child violates the student code of conduct, a meeting is convened with the LEA, parent, and school personnel to determine if the behavior is a result of the disability or not. If yes, the child is removed for 10 days to a separate setting and a functional behavior analysis is performed, if not already done. If no, the school can follow the consequences of breaking the school code for that child and separate the child for not more than 45 calendar days

- Children with disabilities who have been expelled from school still have the right to an education, and the state must guarantee that services are still provided throughout the expulsion. (Bowe, 2008)

- Authority to extend Part C services for infants and toddler services beyond the age of two. The extension allows states to extend services until the child enters kindergarten. Educational components on pre-literacy, numeracy skills, and language must be included in the IFSP. Parents must be notified of the differences between Part C and Part B.

- Short-term objectives and benchmarks are no longer required sections in the IEP. States can determine "the extent to which short-term objectives and benchmarks are used." (Federal register, 2006)

I. INDIVIDUALIZED FAMILY SERVICE PLAN (IFSP) INFORMATION

The information section includes specific data about the child and family. It also has space for listing the IFSP team members. This section can serve as a directory for the team members.

Child's Name: Enter the first, middle, and last name of the child.

Parent's Name: Enter the name(s) of parent(s) or guardian.

Address: Enter street, route, or post office box address(es) of parent(s) or guardian.

City/State: Record city and state.

Day Phone: Enter phone number where parent(s) can be reached during the day.

I. INDIVIDUALIZED FAMILY SERVICE PLAN (IFSP) INFORMATION

Child's Name _____

Parent(s)' Name(s) _____
_____

Address _____

City/State _____

Day
Phone _____   DOB _____   ☐ Male ☐ Female

Evening
Phone _____   Age at Referral _____

County _____   Date of Referral _____

                              IFSP Meeting Date _____

                              IFSP Start Date _____

Zip Code _____   Interim IFSP Date _____ ☐ N/A

IFSP TEAM

Name	Relationship/Role	Phone Number	Address	Date

Language Spoken at Home _____

School District _____

Child's Name _____ ☐ N/A

Medicaid Number _____

Agency _____

Section Number _____

Evening Phone: Enter phone number where parent(s) can be reached during the evening.

County: Enter the child's legal county of residence.

Zip Code: Record zip code.

Date of Birth: Enter month/day/year of child's birth. Date format is mm/dd/yy.

Sex: Check the appropriate box for Male or Female.

Age at Referral: Enter child's chronological age at time of referral to the Infant-Toddler Program.

Date of Referral: Enter month/day/year the child was referred to the Infant-Toddler Program. Date format is mm/dd/yy.

IFSP Meeting Date: Enter the month/day/year the IFSP meeting actually occurred. Date format is mm/dd/yy.

IFSP Start Date: Enter the month/day/year the family signs the IFSP. Date format is mm/dd/yy.

Interim IFSP Date: If this document is an interim IFSP, enter the month/day/year the family signs. Otherwise, check the box for "NA". Date format is mm/dd/yy.

IFSP Team: List the family members' names to be followed by the EI Service Coordinator and other team members. Include guardians, foster, and surrogate parents as team members. Enter the name of the team member, the relationship/role, the phone number, the address, and the date the team member began working with the family.

Language Spoken in Home: Enter the language(s) spoken by the primary caregivers in the home where the child lives.

School District: Enter the school or school district in which the child's current address is located.

Child's Name: Enter the first, middle, and last name of the child.

Medicaid Number: Enter child's Medicaid number. If child does not have a Medicaid number, check the box indicating N/A.

II. FAMILY CONCERNS, PRIORITIES, AND RESOURCES
(Optional, for the family to complete)

Why are you interested in receiving help for your child?

What do you want the IFSP Team to know about your child?

- Pregnancy and birth history
- History of child's growth and development
- Medical Information
- Other important events or information

- When you were first concerned
- Effect of child's needs on the family
- Child likes
- Family activities
- Parent choices
- Your concerns now

- What is most important to you now
- Helpful people and agencies

Date	Information

Child's Name _____

Medicaid Number _____ ☐ N/A

Agency _____

Section Number _____

Agency: Identify which Children's Developmental Services Agency is involved.

Section Number: Identify page using the roman numerals corresponding with the Section. If inserting additional pages, indicate with letter of alphabet after numeral (e.g. if adding a page to Section III, identify that page as IIIa).

II. FAMILY CONCERNS, PRIORITIES, AND RESOURCES (OPTIONAL, FOR THE FAMILY TO COMPLETE)

Including family information in the IFSP is voluntary on the part of the family. This information helps identify what families want from early intervention for their children and themselves.

It is important for the family to express their concerns, priorities, and resources in a positive manner because these elements become the backbone for the rest of the document. This section should be presented to families to complete. Staff should be available to assist by lending encouragement, giving examples, brainstorming, etc. In some instances the EI Service Coordinator may be requested or need to offer to record the family's concerns, priorities, and resources.

Why are you interested in receiving help for your child?
This question is asked because it encourages the family to express their hopes for growth and change. Families may not know what services are available and might respond, "We are not sure; our doctor suggested we come and talk with you". Regardless of the response, it opens discussion and the opportunity to express concerns.

What do you want the team to know about your child?
This section suggests topics for the family to address, and gives them the freedom to choose what they wish to address. The topics are only there to generate discussion and do not pertain to all situations. This is where the family shares their perspective of events in their child's life. Information may point out areas where strengths can be reinforced or assistance is needed. In recounting their stories, families often find new ways of seeing events and recognizing strengths.

If the family elects not to complete this section, the EI Service Coordinator should document on the page that the opportunity was offered and declined at this time.

Date: Use this column to indicate the date the family shares concerns, priorities, and resources and other information. Date format is mm/dd/yy.

III. SUMMARY OF CHILD'S PRESENT ABILITIES AND STRENGTHS

Include a summary of functional assessments, evaluations, and observations of the child in his day-to-day environment. List evaluators, procedures, results, and child's strengths and needs. Address all of the following domains for an initial IFSP.

- Adaptive/self help skills (bathing, feeding, dressing, toileting, etc.)
- Cognitive skills (thinking, reasoning, learning)
- Communication skills (responding, understanding, and using language)

- Physical development (vision, hearing, motor, and health)
- Social/emotional skills (feelings, playing, and interacting)

Date	Description

Child's Name _____

Medicaid Number _____ ☐ N/A

Agency _____

Section Number _____

Information: Record information related by the family pertaining to their concerns, priorities, and resources and other information.

Child's Name: Enter the first, middle, and last name of the child.

Medicaid Number: Enter child's Medicaid number. If child does not have a Medicaid number, check the box indicating N/A.

Agency: Identify which Children's Developmental Services Agency is involved.

Section Number: Identify page using the roman numerals corresponding with the Section. If inserting additional pages, indicate with letter of alphabet after numeral (e.g. if adding a page to Section III, identify that page as IIIa).

III. SUMMARY OF CHILD'S PRESENT ABILITIES AND STRENGTHS

In this section, the results of all evaluations are summarized and discussed by the team for the initial IFSP. Each domain must be addressed for the initial IFSP. It includes the family's observations of the child in his day-to-day environments, medical information, formal evaluations, and other sources of information. The team includes the parent(s), as well as other professionals representing several disciplines, and the EI Service Coordinator. The summary information should be written in simple jargon-free language so that it is clear and understandable to all.

Emphasis should be given to a child's present abilities and strengths within day-to-day routines rather than on developmental levels. This is particularly important since many evaluations compare a child's development to the development of children without disabilities. This section includes information on what the child can do and what he needs to learn. The child's learning style is also described so that natural abilities can be strengthened and built upon. New information about the child's abilities, strengths, and needs should be added as evaluations, assessments, and observations are conducted.

Date: Enter the date the evaluation(s), assessment(s), or observation(s) took place. Date format is mm/dd/yy.

Description: The summary of the team evaluation must include names of evaluators/their titles, assessments used, and statements that describe the child's present status and levels of development in all of the following domains for the initial IFSP:

1. Adaptive/self-help skills (bathing, feeding, dressing, toileting, etc.)

2. Cognitive skills (thinking, reasoning, learning)

3. Communication skills (responding, understanding, and using language)

4. Physical development (vision, hearing, motor, and current health status)

5. Social/emotional skills (feelings, playing, interacting)

Child's Name: Enter the first, middle, and last name of the child.

Medicaid Number: Enter child's Medicaid number. If child does not have a Medicaid number, check the box indicating N/A.

Agency: Identify which Children's Developmental Services Agency is involved.

Section Number: Identify page using the roman numerals corresponding with the Section. If inserting additional pages, indicate with letter of alphabet after numeral (e.g. if adding a page to Section III, identify that page as IIIa).

IV. IFSP OUTCOMES

Outcomes are the changes the family wants for themselves or for their child. Outcomes should be discussed at the IFSP meeting by all team members as related to the family's concerns, priorities, and resources, the child's abilities and needs or both. New outcomes can be added at any time additions are desired or needed.

Family's Concerns, Priorities, and Resources: State the family's concerns along with their priorities and resources when related to the identified outcome.

1. **Concerns** are the areas identified by the family as needs, issues, or problems they want to address.

2. **Priorities** are things or accomplishments important to the family.

3. **Resources** are formal and informal means that can help the family.

IV. IFSP OUTCOMES

Family's Concerns, Priorities, and Resources	Child's Abilities/Needs

Outcome # _____ Start Date _____ Target Date _____

Activities	Person Responsible

Date Reviewed	Outcome Status	Comments on Status

Child's Name _____

Medicaid Number _____ ☐ N/A

Agency _____

Section Number _____

Child's Abilities/Needs: State what the child is able to do and what he needs to be able to do when related to the identified outcome.

Outcome #___: Place the sequential number of the outcome on the line. Then, in the space provided, write a description of the desired end result of what the child or family will do or accomplish. Each subsequent outcome should be numbered consecutively per page in Section IV. Outcomes may be child or family-focused.

Target Date: Enter the anticipated date this outcome will be completed. Enter revised target dates as needed when time frames must be adjusted. Date format is mm/dd/yy.

Start Date: Enter the date that work toward the desired outcome will begin. Date format is mm/dd/yy.

Activities: Describe the methods and procedures that will be used to reach the outcome. Include a projected completion date if desired. Activities should tell the person reading the statement what is being done to achieve the outcome.

Person Responsible: Name the person(s) responsible for carrying out the activities to help the child or family achieve the outcome. Family member(s) may be identified as person(s) responsible.

Dates Reviewed/Outcome Status/Comments:
Enter date outcome progress was reviewed. Next to date, write one of these terms: "achieved", "ongoing", or "discontinued" to describe outcome status at that time. Under comments, explain why an outcome is ongoing or discontinued. Additional review dates and outcome status should be entered as appropriate if prior review status was "ongoing". Date format is mm/dd/yy.

Child's Name: Enter the first, middle, and last name of the child.

Medicaid Number: Enter child's Medicaid number. If child does not have a Medicaid number, check the box indicating N/A.

Agency: Identify which Children's Developmental Services Agency is involved.

Section Number: Identify page using the roman numerals corresponding with the Section. If inserting additional pages, indicate with

V. IFSP SERVICE DELIVERY PLAN

Early Intervention Service	Provider	Projected Start Date	Actual Start Date	Location / Most Natural Environment	Frequency / Intensity / Method	Cost to Family / Payment Arrangement	Anticipated Duration	Date Ended

Other Services	Provider	Funding Source

Primary Place of Service _____

Child's Name _____

Medicaid Number _____ ☐ N/A

Agency _____

Section Number _____

letter of alphabet after numeral (e.g. if adding a page to Section III, identify that page as IIIa).

V. IFSP SERVICE DELIVERY PLAN

The IFSP Service Delivery Plan is intended to help identify important details in carrying out the activities written in the IFSP Outcomes Section IV. The IFSP Service Delivery Plan provides a way to record specific information to explain how, when, where, and under what conditions the early intervention services are expected.

Family members and professionals are encouraged to discuss services openly and to make joint decisions based on the outcomes chosen by the parents or family members. The services should be provided by qualified individuals in the child's natural environment as much as possible. The cost for services to family members is an important matter to be considered in planning services. Use cost information that is available. Expectations about how long the services will be provided are another detail to be discussed. Reaching agreement will help all who have a responsibility identified in the plan to meet family members' expectations and providers' information needs.

Early Intervention Service: Record which of the required services is/are planned. Required services are:

- Assistive Technology Services and Devices
- Audiological Services
- Community Based Rehabilitative Services
- Early Identification and Screening
- Family Counseling and Therapy Services
- Health Services
- Multidisciplinary Evaluations and Assessments
- Medical Services
- Nursing Services
- Nutritional Services
- Occupational Therapy
- Physical Therapy
- Psychological Services
- Respite Services
- Service Coordination/ Targeted Case Management
- Speech/Language Therapy
- Social Work Services
- Transportation
- Vision Services

Provider: Record the agency/organization that will provide the service.

Projected Start Date: Record the month, day, and year the service is planned to begin. Date format is mm/dd/yy.

Actual Date: Record the month, day, and year the service actually begins. Date format is mm/dd/yy.

Location/Most Natural Environment: Record the actual place or places where the service will be provided. To the maximum extent appropriate to the needs of the child, early intervention services must be provided in natural environments including the home and community settings where children without disabilities participate. If the most natural environment is not utilized, indicate this in **Section VI** which is identified as **"Natural Environments/Settings"** and follow instructions for that section.

Frequency/Intensity/Method: Record the number of days or sessions that a service will be provided (e.g., four times a month, once quarterly, two times per week), the length of each session, and whether the service is on an individual or group basis.

Cost to Family/Payment Arrangement: Record the approximate cost of the service to the child's family. The cost is the amount the family will be obligated to pay. The estimated cost should be based on the usual and customary fees charged by the provider and excludes amounts expected to be covered by insurance and sliding fee scale allowances. Put "none" if there is no cost to the family. Sources of payment typically are one or more of the following:

- Private insurance

- Medicaid

- Self-payment

- Other public or private resource

Anticipated Duration: Record the month, day, and year that represents how long the service is expected to occur.

Date Ended: Record the month, day, and year the service was completed. Date format is mm/dd/yy.

Other Services: The IFSP Team must identify other services (e.g. well child care, immunizations) and supports in addition to the ITP services that are needed by the child and family. By including these on the IFSP, a complete, coordinated plan is developed for the child and family. Listing these on the IFSP does not obligate the Infant-Toddler Program to provide or pay for these services. However, Service Coordination should assist the family in accessing these services and identifying funding to pay for these services.

Provider: Record the agency/organization that will provide the service.

Funding Source: Identify how the services will be funded.

Primary Place of Service: Enter location where child primarily receives Early Intervention services.

Child's Name: Enter the first, middle, and last name of the child.

Medicaid Number: Enter child's Medicaid number. If child does not have a Medicaid number, check the box indicating N/A.

Agency: Identify which Children's Developmental Services Agency is involved.

Section Number: Identify page using the roman numerals corresponding with the Section. If inserting additional pages, indicate with letter of alphabet after numeral (e.g. if adding a page to Section III, identify that page as IIIa).

VI. NATURAL ENVIRONMENT/SETTING

Federal statues require that early intervention services be provided in natural environments and may only be provided in other settings when outcomes cannot be achieved satisfactorily in the natural environment. IDEA requires justification to support the IFSP team's decision that the outcome cannot be achieved satisfactorily in the natural environment.

Outcome #: Identify which outcome (by number) cannot be achieved satisfactorily in the natural environment. You may have more than one outcome but answer for each one individually.

Service: List the specific service.

1. Discuss efforts and rationale as to why outcome cannot be met in the natural environment. Provide supportive information from the team. Lack of service providers who are willing to provide services in the natural environment is not a justification, nor is family choice. Justification should specify the rationale for why the setting selected is appropriate for the child.

2. Describe how the intervention will be generalized into the child's and family's daily routines and activities. Provide information about what the service provider, the family, or

VI. NATURAL ENVIRONMENT/SETTING

Federal statutes require that early intervention services be provided in natural environments and may only be provided in other settings when outcomes cannot be achieved satisfactorily in the natural environment. IDEA requires justification to support the IFSP team's decision that the outcome cannot be achieved satisfactorily in the natural environment.

Outcome #	Service	1. Discuss Efforts and Rationale Why Outcome Cannot be Met in Natural Environment	2. Describe How the Intervention will be Generalized into Child's and Family's Daily Routines and Activities	3. Identify Steps for Moving Intervention into a Natural Environment

Child's Name _____

Medicaid Number _____ ☐ N/A

Agency _____

Section Number _____

other caregivers are doing that is consistent with the daily routines and activities. When is intervention occurring in daily routines/activities?

3. Identify steps for moving intervention into a natural environment. Provide intervention strategies for moving from a setting which is not considered natural or typical for the child into a natural environment. Think about gradually moving from one setting to the other, mixing the settings, and eventually getting to all settings that are natural environments.

Child's Name: Enter the first, middle, and last name of the child.

Medicaid Number: Enter child's Medicaid number. If child does not have a Medicaid number, check the box indicating N/A.

Agency: Identify which Children's Developmental Services Agency is involved.

Section Number: Identify page using the roman numerals corresponding with the Section. If inserting additional pages, indicate with letter of alphabet after numeral (e.g. if adding a page to Section III, identify that page as IIIa).

VII. TRANSITION PLANNING

1. Discuss what "transition" from early intervention means.

Families must be informed that the entitlements afforded them and their children under the Infant-Toddler Program's end at the child's third birthday. Discussions should continue throughout the child's enrollment in the Infant-Toddler Program as deemed appropriate. Discuss and educate parents, as early as child's enrollment in the Infant-Toddler Program, on future placements, what "transition" from Infant-Toddler Program means, and what we can do to plan for this transition. Document what the Service Coordinator did to make sure the family had this knowledge and where they documented this.

2. Explore preschool special education services as well as other community program options for the child.

Discuss with the family the preschool special education services and other resources that may be appropriate for their child. Review program options from the child's third birthday through the remainder of the school year. Indicate if this has been done and where it is documented.

VII. TRANSITION PLANNING

Transition Plans and Activities	Specific Action	Person Responsible	Date Started	Date Completed
1. Discuss what "transition" from early intervention means.				
2. Explore preschool special education services as well as other community program options for the child.				
3. Send specified information to Part B and/or other community programs, with parental consent. Yes ☐ No ☐				
4. With parental consent and written prior notice, convene a transition planning conference with all parties required to develop a transition plan and steps.				
5. Help the child begin to learn new skills needed to get along in a new setting. Help the child and family prepare for changes in services.				

Child's Name _____

Medicaid Number _____   ☐ N/A

Agency _____

Section Number _____

3. Send specified information to Part B and/or other community programs, with parental consent.

The family provides consent for release of information to public schools and other programs or services. Check yes if the family gave permission or no if they did not. Explain here what was sent who received the information. Example: assessment reports, IFSP, etc.

4. With parental consent, convene a transition planning conference with all parties required to develop a transition plan and steps.

The meeting(s) can occur as early as nine months prior to the child's third birthday, but must occur no later than 90 days prior to the child's third birthday. Enter each of the date(s) under **Date Completed**. Provide Written Prior Notice of the transition meeting. The following participants must be invited to the transition meeting(s):

- parent

- Local Education Agency representative

- representative of the evaluative agency if the child has been evaluated

- any other person or service providers who might help support & develop the transition plan

5. Help the child begin to learn new skills needed to get along in a new setting. Help the child and family prepare for changes in services.

Document in **Section IV "IFSP Outcomes"** and identify strategies a child may need prior to leaving one program and transitioning to another. How did someone prepare the family and child for these changes? Refer to the specific outcome number where these actions occur.

*Add additional activities as deemed appropriate for individual children and their families under specific actions.

Person Responsible: Name the person(s) responsible for each specific action.

Date Started: Enter the date each activity was projected to start. Date format is mm/dd/yy.

Date Completed: Enter the date each activity was completed. Date format is mm/dd/yy.

Child's Name: Enter the first, middle, and last name of the child.

Medicaid Number: Enter child's Medicaid number. If child does not have a Medicaid number, check the box indicating N/A.

Agency: Identify which Children's Developmental Services Agency is involved.

Section Number: Identify page using the roman numerals corresponding with the Section. If inserting additional pages, indicate with letter of alphabet after numeral (e.g. if adding a page to Section III, identify that page as IIIa)

VIII. IFSP AGREEMENT

The family is a consumer of early intervention services and should be involved in developing the IFSP. The contents of the IFSP must be fully explained and the agreement statement must be reviewed. The parent or guardian should be informed that his signature will indicate:

- Participation in developing the plan
- Advisement on all services and costs involved
- Choice to accept or reject any specific service(s) or the entire plan
- Right to change decision at any time
- Awareness of IFSP distribution
- Agreement with the plan

Comments/concerns I wish to add: The parent may record any additional information, concerns, or differences.

Signatures: The parent or guardian's legal rights are recognized by asking for his signature. The parent or guardian signs and dates where indicated. The EI Service Coordinator and Provider Agency Representatives or their Designees sign and date where indicated acknowledging their agreement to work with the family and service providers to ensure availability of services listed in this IFSP.

Child's Name: Enter the first, middle, and last name of the child.

Medicaid Number: Enter child's Medicaid number. If child does not have a Medicaid number, check the box indicating N/A.

Agency: Identify which Children's Developmental Services Agency is involved.

VIII. IFSP AGREEMENT

Comments/concerns I wish to add:

I have received a copy of the Child and Family Rights under Part C of IDEA. These rights have been explained to me and I understand them. I participated in the development of this IFSP, and I give informed consent for the North Carolina Infant-Toddler Program and service providers to carry out the activity or activities listed on this IFSP.

Consent means: I have been fully informed about the activity or activities for which consent is sought; I was informed in my native language (unless clearly not feasible to do so) or other mode of communication; and I understand and agree in writing to the implementation of the activity or activities for which consent is sought; the consent describes that activity or activities; and the granting of my consent is voluntary and may be revoked in writing at any time.

I understand that I may decline a service or services without jeopardizing any other early intervention service(s) my child or family receive through the North Carolina Infant-Toddler Program. I understand that my IFSP will become a part of my child's NC Infant-Toddler Program record and shared with service providers implementing this IFSP.

Parent/Guardian Signature	Date
EI Service Coordinator Signature/Agency	Date
Other Signature	Date

Parent/Guardian Signature	Date
Agency Representative or Designee Signature/Agency	Date
Other Signature	Date

Child's Name _____

Medicaid Number _____ ☐ N/A

Agency _____

Section Number _____

Section Number: Identify page using the roman numerals corresponding with the Section. If inserting additional pages, indicate with letter of alphabet after numeral (e.g. if adding a page to Section III, identify that page as IIIa).

IX. IFSP REVIEW

This section is to be used any time there is an IFSP review. It is not necessary to wait until a Semi-Annual or Annual Review to review the plan and make changes that are needed or desired by the family. Three (3) kinds of IFSP reviews are:

- **Semi-Annual**
- **Annual**
- **Other reviews (at the family's request)**

Review Date: Enter the month, day, and year the review takes place. Date format is mm/dd/yy.

Summarize Review Results: There are times when reviews are not conducted as scheduled. If this should occur, note the reasons why a review is not conducted on schedule. If the family foregoes the review, the EI Service Coordinator should convene a review meeting with the other service providers to document that the review has occurred. The family and service providers are encouraged to make comments in this section related to:

- Progress being made toward achieving outcomes
- The family's satisfaction with services being received
- Any new and relevant information related to the child and family
- The results of any evaluations and assessments conducted
- Plans until the next scheduled review
- At Annual Review, whether this IFSP will continue or a new IFSP will be developed
- Team members who were present
- How team members not present contributed to the review

Review Cycle: Check the space that corresponds to the kind of review. Use a new Section VII every time there is a review.

IX. IFSP REVIEW

Review Date	Summarize Review Results

REVIEW CYCLE ☐ Semi-Annual ☐ Annual ☐ Other _____ Target Date for Next Review _____

I have participated in the review of this IFSP and give informed consent for the NC Infant-Toddler Program and its service providers to carry out any changes in the activity or activities listed on this IFSP Review. The rights under the Infant-Toddler Program have been reviewed and explained to me and I understand them. A copy of the Parent Handbook for the Infant-Toddler Program has been given to me.

Consent means: I have been fully informed about the activity or activities for which consent is sought; I was informed in my native language (unless clearly not feasible to do so) or other mode of communication; and I understand and agree in writing to the implementation of the activity or activities for which consent is sought; the consent describes that activity or activities; and the granting of my consent is voluntary and may be revoked in writing at any time.

Parent/Guardian Signature	Date
EI Service Coordinator Signature/Agency	Date
Other Signature	Date

Parent/Guardian Signature	Date
Agency Representative or Designee Signature/Agency	Date
Other Signature	Date

Child's Name _____

Medicaid Number _____ ☐ N/A

Agency _____

Section Number _____

For Annual IFSP Review:

The latest copy of the Parent Handbook for the NC Infant-Toddler Program has been offered to me

Initial here _____

Target Date for Next Review: Record the date when the next review will be conducted. A review of the IFSP is to occur every six months following the date of the signing of the Initial IFSP. If a review is delayed, the next review should occur on schedule from the date of the signing of the Initial IFSP, even if a full six months has not elapsed. Date format is mm/dd/yy.

Signatures: Enter the signatures of the EI Service Coordinator, the parents and parent surrogates who are present at the review meeting. A parent signature indicates informed consent and understanding of Child and Family Rights under the NC Infant-Toddler Program. Additionally, a parent initials for latest copy of the NC Parent Handbook at the annual IFSP Review.

Child's Name: Enter the first, middle, and last name of the child.

Medicaid Number: Enter child's Medicaid number. If child does not have a Medicaid number, check the box indicating N/A.

Agency: Identify which Children's Developmental Services Agency is involved.

Section Number: Identify page using the roman numerals corresponding with the Section. If inserting additional pages, indicate with letter of alphabet after numeral (e.g. if adding a page to Section III, identify that page as IIIa).

Available from http://www.ncei.org. Each state has a link to IFSP forms. The one presented here is for North Carolina.

3

TYPES OF EXCEPTIONALITIES

AUTISM AND RELATED DISORDERS

Federal definition: "Autism means a developmental disability significantly affecting verbal and nonverbal communication and social interaction, generally evident before age three that adversely affects a child's educational performance. Other characteristics often associated with autism are engagement in repetitive activities and stereotyped movements, resistance to environmental change or change in daily routines, and unusual responses to sensory experiences." [34 Code of Federal Regulations §300.8(c)(1).]

CHECKLIST FOR AUTISM IN TODDLERS (CHAT)

The following test can be used by a pediatrician or family doctor during the 18-month developmental check-up. The CHAT should not be used as a diagnostic instrument but can alert the primary health professional to the need for an expert referral.

Yes	No	
Yes	**No**	I. During the appointment, has the child made eye contact with you?
Yes	**No**	*ii. Get the child's attention, then point across the room at an interesting object and say, "Oh look! There's a (name of toy)!" Watch the child's face. Does the child look across to see what your are pointing at? *(1)*
Yes	**No**	*iii. Get the child's attention, then give child a miniature toy cup and teapot and say, "Can you make a cup of tea?" (Substitute toy pitcher and glass and say, "Can you pour a glass of juice?") Does the child pretend to pour out tea (juice), drink it, etc? *(2)*
Yes	**No**	*iv. Say to the child, "Where's the light?", or "Show me the light. "Does the child POINT with his/her index finger at the light? *(3)*
Yes	**No**	v. Can the child build a tower of bricks (blocks)? (If so how many?) (Number of bricks....)

* Indicates critical questions that are most indicative of autistic characteristics.

1. To record YES on this item, ensure the child has not simply looked at your hand, but has actually looked at the object you are pointing at.

2. If you can elicit an example of pretending in some other game, score a YES on this item.

3. Repeat this with, "Where's the Teddy Bear?" or some other unreachable object; if child does not understand the word "light". To record a YES on this item, the child must have looked up at your face around the time of pointing.

Sources: The British Journal of Psychiatry, 1996, vol 168, pp. 158–163.
The British Journal of Psychiatry, 1992, vol 161, pp. 839–843.

BOOKS FOR TEACHERS

1001 Great Ideas for Teaching or Raising Children with Autism Spectrum Disorders by Veronica Zysk, Ellen Notbohm. Future Horizons, Inc., 2004.
Just as it says, 1001 great ideas for teaching children with Autism.

Children with Special Needs in Early Childhood Settings by Carol L. Paashce, Lola Gorill, and Bev Strom. Thomson Delmar Learning, 2004.
A great resource for every teacher of young children. This handbook has resources, websites, ideas, and characteristics to look for as you observe young children in the classroom.

Playing, Laughing and Learning with Children on the Autism Spectrum by Julia Moor. Jessica Kingsley Publishers, 2002.
This book shows you how to break activities down into manageable steps so even the most severs child can be successful and independent.

The TEACCH Approach to Autism Spectrum Disorders by Gary B. Mesibov, Eric Schopler, Victoria Shea. Springer-Verlag New York, LLC, 2004.
The TEACCH approach is fully explained in lay terms for all teachers to be able to begin to teach children with Autism.

You're Going to Love This Kid: Teaching Students with Autism in the Inclusive Classroom by Paula Kluth. Paul H. Brookes, 2003.
Strategies for inclusion are shared as you work through the text.

BOOKS FOR PARENTS

George and Sam: Two Boys, One Family and Autism by Charlotte Moore. St. Martins Press, 2006.
This is a mother's tale of raising not one but two boys with Autism and one without. She shares her joys, struggles and tears.

Let Me Hear Your Voice: A Family's Triumph over Autism by Catherine Maurice.Random House, Inc. 1994.
A mother's tale from diagnosis to treatment is told with a sense of hope.

A Parent's Guide to Asperger Syndrome and High-Functioning Autism: How to Meet the Challenges and Help Your Child Thrive by Geraldine Dawson, Sally Ozonoff. Guilford Publications, Inc, 2002.
This book presents ideas for parents that have been proven to work with children with Autism.

Raising a Child with Autism by Shira Richman. Jessica Kingsley Publishers, 2001.
Richman describes how to use the Applied Behavior Approach in the home, including working with siblings, dressing independence, and eating habits.

Ten Things Every Child with Autism Wishes You Knew by Ellen Notbohm. Future Horizons, Inc., 2005.
Sharing personal stories, the author invites you into the world of the Autistic mind.

WEBSITES

Autism Society of America
http://www.autism-society.org/
This site provides information to help people understand autism and is a support for family resources as well.

Autism Web
http://www.autismweb.com/
This website is designed specifically for parents to unlock the mystery of autism.

Center for the Study of Autism
http://www.autism.org/
Different research methods are presented and debated on this website so parents can be informed about how best to proceed with their child.

Reaching Potentials

http://www.reachingpotentials.org
This is a non-profit organization that provides services to autistic children and families.

TEACCH

http://www.teacch.com/
TEACCH stands for Treatment and Education of Autistic and Related Communication-handicapped Children. This website provides links to up-to-date research and programs related to autism.

LEARNING DISABILITIES

Federal Definition: "A disorder in one or more of the basic psychological processes involved in understanding or in using language, spoken or written, that may manifest itself in an imperfect ability to listen, think, speak, read, write, spell, or do mathematical calculations, including conditions such as perceptual disabilities, brain injury, minimal brain dysfunction, dyslexia, and developmental aphasia."

However, learning disabilities do not include, "...learning problems that are primarily the result of visual, hearing, or motor disabilities, of mental retardation, of emotional disturbance, or of environmental, cultural, or economic disadvantage." [34 Code of Federal Regulations §300.7(c)(10)]

There is not just one sign of a problem with children who have learning disabilities. Sometimes there could be many. A few to draw your attention to are:

- Children who have trouble remembering what has just been read to them

- Children who cannot follow simple one-step directions

- Children who have difficulty spelling their name

- Children who cannot remember their letters or numbers

- Children who seem to be behind others their age both cognitively and academically

BOOKS FOR TEACHERS

Complete Learning Disabilities Handbook: *Ready-to-Use Strategies & Activities for Teaching Students with Learning Disabilities* by Joan M. Harwell. Wiley, John & Sons, Inc., 2001.
A must-have for any teacher of children with learning disabilities. It includes a tool-kit and ideas for the at-risk child.

The Inclusive Early Childhood Classroom by Patti Gould and Joyce Sullivan. Gryphon House, Inc., 1999.
Helping children in all areas of the classroom can often be a challenge. Look inside this book for a wealth of ideas.

It's so Much Work to Be Your Friend: Helping the Child with Learning Disabilities Find Social Success by Richard Lavoie. Simon & Schuster Adult Publishing Group, 2005.
Real life strategies are presented to help the child with learning disabilities interact socially with the peers and adults in their life.

Learning Outside the Lines: Two Ivy League Students with Learning Disabilities and ADHD Give You the Tools for Academic Success and Educational Revolution by Jonathan Mooney, David Cole. Simon & Schuster Adult Publishing Group, 2000.
Written by two students with learning disabilities, provides practical ideas for writing papers, studying for tests, and following directions.

Thank You, Mr. Falker by Patricia Polacco. Penguin Young Readers Group, 1998.
Even though this is story book for children, teachers can read it and appreciate the struggle from within.

BOOKS FOR PARENTS

All Kinds of Minds: A Young Student's Book About Learning Abilities and Learning Disorders by Mel Levine. Educators Publishing Service, Inc., 1992.
Students with learning disabilities learn differently. This book helps them feel a part of the world where they are no longer alone.

The Everything Parent's Guide to Children With Dyslexia by Abigail Marshall. Adams Media Corporation, 2004.
Need help reading with your child? This book will give you tips for IEP goals and objectives.

The Misunderstood Child: Understanding and Coping with Your Child's Learning Disabilities by Larry B. Silver. Crown Publishing Group, 2006. This is a resource for all parents of children with disabilities. It has up-to-date research and online resources.

The Myth of Laziness by Mel Levine. Simon & Schuster Adult Publishing Group, 2004.
Have you been told your child is just lazy? You know that is not true, but how do you prove it?

A Special Education: One Family's Journey Through the Maze of Learning Disabilities by Dana Buchman, Charlotte Farber. Da Capo Press, 2006.
A mother and daughter share their struggles with learning about each other and how to cope with learning disabilities.

WEBSITES

LD Online
http://www.ldonline.org/
This is an interactive resource for parents, children, and teachers.

Learning Disabilities of America
http://www.ldanatl.org/
This is more than an organization that you can join. It is a resource for parents and teachers. Remember, just because you have a learning disability doesn't mean you can't do anything you try.

Kids Source
http://www.kidsource.com/
Do the types of learning disabilities overwhelm and confuse you? Use this site to answer many questions. Once on the site search by learning disabilities.

National Center for Learning Disabilities
http://www.ncld.org/
Research is posted here keeping parents and teachers current on learning disabilities, their causes, and treatments.

National Dissemination Center for Children with Disabilities (NICHCY)—Disability Info: Learning Disabilities
http://www.nichcy.org/
This site opens with a child's story and then proceeds into questions and answers. On the site you can search by disability information. There are fact sheets by most categories.

COGNITIVE DISABILITIES (MENTAL RETARDATION)

Federal definition: "Significantly sub average general intellectual functioning, existing concurrently with deficits in adaptive behavior and manifested during the developmental period that adversely affects a child's educational performance." [34 Code of Federal Regulations §300.7(c)(6).]

Causes of Cognitive Disabilities: There are many reasons a person may have cognitive disabilities. A few are listed below:

- Health concerns–illnesses such as bacterial meningitis can leave as a lasting effect mental retardation. The illness causes fluid build-up on the brain resulting in lack of functioning.

- Genetics–Down Syndrome is a genetic complication when there are three chromosomes on number 21.

- Environmental–Lead poisoning can cause brain damage leading to mental retardation.

- Birthing process–During birth, a lack of oxygen to the brain may lead to a child's having mental retardation.

To determine the severity of the cognitive disability, an IQ test is performed. Based upon the score, the child is labeled as mild (60–80), moderate (40–60), severe (20–40) or profound (20 and below). An adaptive behavior scale is also evaluated for each child. Both scores together help in planning goals for the child.

BOOKS FOR TEACHERS

Babies with Down Syndrome: A New Parents' Guide by Karen Stray-Gunderson (Editor). Woodbine House, 1995.
You have just learned that a baby with Down Syndrome will be in your class on Monday. What will you do?

Fine Motor Skills in Children with Down Syndrome: A Guide for Parents and Professionals by Maryanne Bruni. Woodbine House, 2006.
Help these children become successful in life by using these strategies.

Gross Motor Skills in Children with Down Syndrome: A Guide for Parents and Professionals by Patricia C. Winders. Woodbine House, 1997.
Children with Down Syndrome learn gross motor skills but need help in refining them. This book opens those doors.

OUACHITA TECHNICAL COLLEGE

Steps to independence: Teaching everyday skills to children with special needs (4th ed.) by Bruce Baker & Alan Brightman. Paul H. Brookes, 2004.
A must have resource with everyday tips to help a child learn and develop.

Teaching Reading to Children with Down Syndrome: A Guide for Parents and Teachers by Patricia Logan Oelwein. Woodbine House, 1995.
A tried and true method to helping the child with mental retardation learn to read.

BOOKS FOR PARENTS

Early Communication Skills for Children with Down Syndrome: A Guide for Parents and Professionals, Vol. 1 by Libby Kumin. Woodbine House, 2003.
This book will help parents communicate with their child and open their world.

Parent's Guide to Down Syndrome: Toward a Brighter Future by Siegfried M. Pueschel. Paul H. Brookes, 2001.
The future is still bright, learn how.

Retarded isn't stupid, Mom! (Rev. ed.) by S. Kaufman. Paul H. Brookes, 1999.
This book deals with the anger, frustration, and denial a parent feels as she learns of the diagnosis and the amount she learns from her daughter.

Special Kids Need Special Parents: A Resource for Parents of Children with Special Needs by Judith Loseff Lavin. Penguin Group, 2001.
A wonderful resource for parents to help them help their child.

You Will Dream New Dreams: Inspiring Personal Stories by Parents of Children with Disabilities by Parents of Children with Disabilities by Stanley D. Klein, Kim Schive. Kensington Publishing Corp., 2001.
A book by parents for parents. You are not alone!

WEBSITES

The Arc of the United States
www.thearc.org and www.TheArcPub.com *(Publications)*
Resources for parents and teachers are available on this website. You can also join online communities and find local support chapters.

American Association on Intellectual and Developmental Disabilities (formerly the American Association on Mental Retardation, AAMR)
www.aaidd.org/
Fact sheets, publications, and articles are available. Some are free, and some must be purchased.

Division on Developmental Disabilities
www.dddcec.org
Looking for good research, search no further. This website is kept current with new ideas and position papers.

National Dissemination Center for Children with Disabilities (NICHCY) Disability Info: Mental Retardation
http://www.nichcy.org/
Questions are answered and practical suggestions given on this website. On the site you can search by disability information. There are fact sheets by most categories.

BEHAVIOR DISORDERS INCLUDING ADD AND ADHD

Federal definition: "A condition exhibiting one or more of the following characteristics over a long period of time and to a marked degree that adversely affects a child's educational performance–

(A) An inability to learn that cannot be explained by intellectual, sensory, or health factors.

(B) An inability to build or maintain satisfactory interpersonal relationships with peers and teachers.

(C) Inappropriate types of behavior or feelings under normal circumstances.

(D) A general pervasive mood of unhappiness or depression.

(E) A tendency to develop physical symptoms or fears associated with personal or school problems." [34 Code of Federal Regulations §300.7(c)(9).]

As defined by the IDEA, "emotional disturbance includes schizophrenia but does not apply to children who are socially maladjusted, unless it is determined that they have an emotional disturbance." [34 Code of Federal Regulations §300.7(c)(9).]

ADD/ADHD: "Having limited strength, vitality, or alertness, including a heightened alertness to environmental stimuli that results in limited alertness with respect to the educational environment that is due to chronic or acute health problems such as asthma, attention deficit disorder, or attention deficit hyperactivity disorder, diabetes, epilepsy, a heart condition, hemophilia, lead poisoning, leukemia, nephritis, rheumatic fever, and sickle cell anemia, and that adversely affects a child's educational performance". [34 Code of Federal Regulations §300.7(c)(9).]

What to look for:

- Hyperactivity (short attention span, impulsiveness)

- Aggression/self-injurious behavior (acting out, fighting)

- Withdrawal (failure to initiate interaction with others; retreat from exchanges of social interaction, excessive fear or anxiety)

- Immaturity (inappropriate crying, temper tantrums, poor coping skills)

- Learning difficulties (academically performing below grade level)

Children with the most serious emotional disturbances may exhibit distorted thinking, excessive anxiety, bizarre motor acts, and abnormal mood swings. Some are identified as children who have a severe psychosis or schizophrenia.

BOOKS FOR TEACHERS

1-2-3 Magic: Effective Discipline for Children 2–12 by Thomas W. Phelan. Parentmagic, Inc., 2003.
Discipline without yelling or pain is described in a positive, easy to read format.

From Chaos to Calm: Effective Parenting for Challenging Children with ADHD and Other Behavioral Problems by Janet E. Heininger and Sharon K. Weiss. Penguin Group, 2001.
Consistent discipline, dealing with overreacting, and forgetting are all key components to this text.

A Handbook of Play Therapy with Aggressive Children by David Crenshaw and John Mordock. Jason Aronson Publishers, 2005.
Practical techniques for working with children who are aggressive.

Healing ADD: The Breakthrough Program That Allows You to See and Heal the Six Types of Attention Deficit Disorder by Daniel G. Amen. Penguin Group, 2002.
Not all children with ADD are the same. This book explores at least six different ways and how to work with each type.

Mastering Anger & Aggression: The Brazelton Way by T. Berry Brazelton. Da Capo Press, 2005.
Helpful hints to deal with the biter and the aggressive child are given in this text.

BOOKS FOR PARENTS

10 Days to a Less Defiant Child: The Breakthrough Program for Parents Seeking to Overcome Your Child's Difficult Behavior by Jeffrey Bernstein. Avalon Publishing Group, 2006.
Parents can take back their life and help their child at the same time in about 10 days.

Difficult Child by Stanley Turecki and Leslie Tonner. Bantam Books, 2000.
Tips for parents who have a difficult child.

The Explosive Child by Ross W. Greene. HarperCollins Publishers, 1999.
Do you have an explosive child? This book offers strategies and hope.

Transforming the Difficult Child: The Nurtured Heart Approach by Howard Glasser and Jennifer Easley. Center for the Difficult Child, 1999.
This book will help a parent with their child without the means of medication.

Your Defiant Child: Eight Steps to Better Behavior by Russell A. Barkley and Christine M. Benton. Guilford Publications, Inc., 1998.

Help for working with your child is offered in this text. The eight steps are easy to follow.

WEBSITES

Attention Deficit Disorder Association
www.add.org
Resources, information, and general support.

CH.A.D.D. (Children and Adults with Attention-Deficit/ Hyperactivity Disorder)
www.chadd.org
Parents are not alone, and this website makes them feel that they can handle anything.

The Difficult Child
http://difficultchild.com/
This site pairs with the book (see previous section) nicely and also offers a free online newsletter.

National Dissemination Center for Children with Disabilities (NICHCY)—Disability Info: Mental Retardation
http://www.nichcy.org/
Questions are answered and practical suggestions given on this website. On the site you can search by disability information. There are fact sheets by most categories.

Raising Difficult Children
http://www.difficultchildren.org/
This site has groups that parents can join to get the support they need in working with their child.

COMMUNICATION DISORDERS

American Speech and Language Association (ASHA) definition: "the abnormal acquisition, comprehension, or expression of spoken or written language. The disorder may involve all, one, or some of the phonologic, morphologic, semantic, syntactic, or pragmatics components of the linguistic system. Individuals with language disorders frequently have trouble in sentence processing or in abstracting information meaningfully for storage and retrieval from long term memory." (ASHA, 1980, pp. 317–318)

What to look for:

- **Phonology**—slow development of use of sound, inability to retain from day to day

- **Morphology**—grammatical errors increase instead of decrease, poor use of pronouns

- **Semantics**—slow vocabulary production, lack of verb usage

- **Pragmatics**—trouble engaging in conversations with peers, difficulty interpreting tone

BOOKS FOR TEACHERS

Childhood Speech, Language and Listening Problems, 2nd Edition by Patricia McAleer Hamaguchi. Wiley, John & Sons, Inc., 2001.
A practical guide to help children continue developing their language skills.

Helping Children With Dyspraxia by Maureen Boon. Jessica Kingsley Publishers, 2001.
Teachers are encouraged to be active participants in the child's therapy throughout this text. Check it out!

Language Disorders in Children: Real Families, Real Issues, and Real Interventions by Ellen Morris Tiegerman-Farber, Christine Radziewicz. Pearson Education, 2007.
Real-life interventions are explained for parents and professionals to use.

New Language of Toys: Teaching Communication Skills to Children with Special Needs—a Guide for Parents and Teachers by Sue Schwartz. Woodbine House, 2004.
This explores the approach of using toys to get children to communicate.

Teach Me How to Say It Right: Helping Your Child With Articulation Problems by Dorothy P. Dougherty. New Harbinger Publications, 2005.
Activities are presented here to help all who work with the child understand how sounds are produced and how to get the child to "play" along with you.

BOOKS FOR PARENTS

Beyond Baby Talk: From Sounds to Sentences, A Parent's Complete Guide to Language Development by Kenn Apel Ph.D. and Janet Gallant. Crown Publishing Group, 2001.
If you are having trouble with your child's language, this is the book for you.

Childhood Speech, Language, and Listening Problems: What Every Parent Should Know (Paperback) by Patricia McAleer Hamaguchi. John Wiley Sons, Inc., 1995.
This takes a hands-on approach to help parents work with their child.

Does My Child Have a Speech Problem? by Katherine L. Martin. Chicago Review Press, 1997.
This text addresses the six most common speech and language disorders and gives real-life applications for parents to help their child.

The Late Talker: What to Do If Your Child Isn't Talking Yet by Marilyn C. Agin, Malcolm J. Nicholl and Lisa Geng. St. Martin's Press, 2004.
Answers to parents' questions about late talkers.

One Voice printed by The National Stuttering Association. NSA., 2006.
Personal stories from teens, parents, and professionals about stuttering.

WEBSITES

American Speech-Language-Hearing Association (ASHA)
http://www.asha.org
Lists of professionals as well as links to other specific organizations that help individuals with speech and language disorders.

Cleft Palate Foundation
http://www.cleftline.org/
If you need more information on this disorder, look no further. It has everything you need to answer almost any question related to cleft palates.

National Stuttering Association (NSA)
http://www.nsastutter.org
A wealth of information for parents and professionals to help children who stutter.

Speech Delay.com
http://www.speechdelay.com
This is another website full of resources for parents and professionals to improve the life of children with disabilities.

Voices Association, Inc.
http://www/4voices.org
This is an organization begun by two parents of a child with apraxia who needed a place to find support. It provides testimonials and resources for parents and professionals.

DEAF AND HARD OF HEARING

Federal definition: "An impairment in hearing, whether permanent or fluctuating, that adversely affects a child's educational performance. Deafness is defined as a hearing impairment that is so severe that the child is impaired in processing linguistic information through hearing, with or without amplification." (NICHCY, 2004)

What to look for:

- Difficulty learning vocabulary, grammar, word order, idiomatic expressions, and other aspects of verbal communication

- Failure to respond to their name

- Lack of understanding verbal directions

- Use of more gestures than words

- Lack of facial expression in response to spoken words

- Pulling or tugging on ears

- Uncontrollable crying and holding of ears

BOOKS FOR TEACHERS

Care and Education of a Deaf Child by Pamela Knight and Ruth Swanwick. Multilingual Matters Ltd., 1999.
Terms are defined and practical issues are explored.

Helping Children Who Are Deaf: Family and Community Support for Children Who Do Not Hear Well by Sandy Niemann, Devorah Greenstein and Darlena David. The Hesperian Foundation, 2004.
Families often turn to the child's teacher for support, and the teacher is often at a loss. This book provides a resource of possible community services to aid parents.

Sensational Kids: Hope and Help For Children With Sensory Processing Disorder by Lucy Jane Miller and Doris A. Fuller, Penguin Group, 2006.
Gives ideas for working with a child with auditory processing.

Sign Language for Everyone: A Basic Course in Communication with the Deaf by Cathy Rice. Nelson Books, 2005.
Signs are shown and proper etiquette for working with those in the deaf community are covered.

When the Brain Can't Hear: Unraveling the Mystery of Auditory Processing Disorder by Teri James Bellis. Simon & Schuster Adult Publishing Group, 2003.
Auditory processing is hard to understand and deal with. This book helps explain the ins and outs.

BOOKS FOR PARENTS

Can You Hear a Rainbow?: The Story of a Deaf Boy Named Chris by Jamee Riggio Heelan. Peachtree Publishers, 2002.
This is the story of a boy who is deaf, his trials and successes, and where he found hope.

Choices in Deafness: A Parents' Guide to Communication Options (Rev.) by A. J. Nair. Woodbine House, 2007.
Questions from assessment to diagnosis are answered here.

Literacy and Your Deaf Child: What Every Parent Should Know by David A. Stewart and Bryan R. Clarke. Gallaudet University Press, 2003.
Do you need help teaching your child to read? Open this book and find the answer.

The Silent Garden: Raising Your Deaf Child (Rev. ed.) by Paul W. Ogden. Gallaudet University Press, 1996.
Parents are shown the wonderful possibilities that await their child.

When Your Child is Deaf: A Guide for Parents (2nd ed.) by David M. Luterman and Antonia Maxon. York Press, 2002.
Another guide for parents who have deaf children.

WEBSITES

Alexander Graham Bell Association for the Deaf and Hard of Hearing
http://www.agbell.org
A place to go for up-to-date resources and materials.

American Society for Deaf Children
http://www.deafchildren.org
One of the founding organizations that helps parents find resources for their child who is hard of hearing.

Laurent Clerc National Deaf Education Center
http://clerccenter.gallaudet.edu/
Part of Gallaudet University, resources are made available to the public regarding deaf education. Once there, search for Laurent Clerc Center.

National Dissemination Center for Children with Disabilities (NICHCY)
Disability Info: Mental Retardation
http://www.nichcy.org/
Questions are answered and practical suggestions given on this website. On the site you can search by disability information. There are fact sheets by most categories.

Self Help for Hard of Hearing People (SHHH)
http://www.hearingloss.org
This website provides links to conventions and other outreach resources for the deaf and hard of hearing.

BLIND OR VISUALLY IMPAIRED

Federal definition: "There are many parts to the definition since there are varying levels of sightedness."

'Partially sighted' indicates some type of visual problem has resulted in a need for special education;

'Low vision' generally refers to a severe visual impairment, not necessarily limited to distance vision. Low vision applies to all individuals with sight who are unable to read the newspaper at a normal viewing distance, even with the aid of eyeglasses or contact lenses. They use a combination of vision and other senses to learn, although they may require adaptations in lighting or the size of print, and, sometimes, braille;

'Legally blind' indicates that a person has less than 20/200 vision in the better eye or a very limited field of vision (20 degrees at its widest point); and totally blind students learn via braille or other non-visual media.

Visual impairment is the consequence of a functional loss of vision, rather than the eye disorder itself. Eye disorders which can lead to visual impairments can include retinal degeneration, albinism, cataracts, glaucoma, muscular problems that result in visual disturbances, corneal disorders, diabetic retinopathy, congenital disorders, and infection. (NICHCY, 2004)

What to look for:

- Difficulty playing with toys because they cannot see them

- Failure to respond to visual stimulation

- Lack of understanding written directions

- Squinting

- Lack of facial expression in response to another's facial expression, such as a smile

- Rubbing eyes

BOOKS FOR TEACHERS

Including Children with Visual Impairment in Mainstream Schools: A Practical Guide by Pauline Davis. Taylor and Francis, Inc., 2003.
A perfect fit for teachers of children with visual impairments.

Seeing eye to eye: An administrator's guide to students with low vision by S. Lewis & C. B. Allman. American Foundation for the Blind, 2000.
Terminology is explained and ideas are suggested for administrators and teachers.

Teaching Social Skills to Students with Visual Impairments: From Theory to Practice edited by Sharon Z. Sacks, Ph. D. and Karen E. Wolffe, Ph.D. American Foundation for the Blind, 2006.
Teachers can find insight into teaching social skills through this text.

When You Have a Visually Impaired Student in Your Classroom—3 title set American Foundation for the Blind, 2005.
This three-title set provides many activities to work with the child in your classroom. A must-have for all teachers of the visually impaired.

Working with Young Children Who Are Blind or Visually Impaired and Their Families, edited by Diane L. Fazzi, PhD., COMS and Rona L. Pogrund, PhD., COMS. American Foundation for the Blind, 2002. Provides information for early intervention for parents and teachers.

BOOKS FOR PARENTS

Children with Visual Impairments: A Parents' Guide, edited by M. Cay Holbrook. Woodbine House, Inc., 1996.
A must have for all parents. All pertinent topics are covered in an easy to read format.

Games for People with Sensory Impairments: Strategies for Including Individuals of All Ages by Lauren J. Lieberman and Jim F. Cowart. Human Kinetics Publishers, 1996.
Games are wonderful for family time. This book explores how to have game night with your child who has a visual impairment.

I'm Cavitt, I'm Two, and I'm Blind! by William F. Cavitt. Authorhouse, 2005.
A personal story of raising a child who is blind is shared.

Learning through Touch: Supporting Children with Visual Impairments and Additional Difficulties by Mike McLinden and Stephen McCall. Taylor and Francis, Inc., 2002.
Helping your child discover their world through the sense of touch is the focus of this book.

Look at It This Way: Toys and Activities for Children with Visual Impairment by Roma Lear. Butterworth-Heinemann, 1998.
Never know what to buy your child? This book is full of toys and activities for your child to play with and learn from.

WEBSITES

American Foundation for the Blind (AFB)
http://www.afb.org
Information for free as well as purchase on all areas for those who are blind.

Blind Children's Resource Center
http://www.blindchildren.org
Full of resources, this is a must-save on your favorites. It has a newsletter, information, and ideas for parents and teachers.

National Association for Parents of the Visually Impaired, Inc.
http://www.napvi.org
This is a resource specifically for parents. Parent advocacy groups have found this site to be most helpful.

National Federation of the Blind (NFB)
http://www.nfb.org
This organization helps parents and children get their needs met. They also have a newsletter and plan conferences.

Resources for Parents and Teachers of Blind Kids
http://www.BrailleSuperstore.com/
Looking for ideas for your child's birthday or holiday?

PHYSICAL DISABILITIES

Federal definition: "'Orthopedically impaired' means having a severe orthopedic impairment. The term includes impairments caused by congenital anomaly, an impairment caused by disease, and an impairment from any other cause." (IDEA, 1990, Sec. 300.6[6])

"Other health impaired" means having limited strength, vitality, or alertness, due to chronic or acute health problems such as heart condition, tuberculosis, rheumatic fever, nephritis, asthma, sickle cell anemia, hemophilia, epilepsy, lead poisoning, leukemia, or diabetes." (Amendments to IDEA, 1990, Sec. 300.5[7])

What to do in your classroom:

- Investigate technological advances—use technology often and everywhere.

- Examine the classroom for mobility issues—can a wheelchair travel through the classroom uninhibited?

- Become comfortable with communication devices such as communication boards, eye gazing systems, and speech synthesizers

BOOKS FOR TEACHERS

Cerebral Palsy: A Complete Guide for Caregiving by Freeman Miller and Steven J. Bachrach. Johns Hopkins University Press, 2006.
As it says, a complete guide to working with children who have cerebral palsy and meeting all their needs.

Inclusive Physical Activity: A Lifetime of Opportunities by Susan l. Kasser and Rebecca K. Lytle. Human Kinetics Publishers, 2005.
This book looks at physical activity throughout life and how people with disabilities can participate and live fulfilling lives.

Sensory Stimulation: Sensory-Focused Activities for People with Physical and Multiple Disabilities by Susan Fowler. Jessica Kingsley Publishers, 2006.
Children with physical disabilities are often left out of sensorial work because it is felt that they cannot use their senses well. This book challenges that and provides solutions.

Teaching Motor Skills to Children With Cerebral Palsy and Similar Movement Disorders: A Guide for Parents and Professionals by Sieglinde Martin. Woodbine House, 2006.
Exercises for children with cerebral palsy are described so that daily therapy is not such a chore.

Teaching Students With Medical, Physical, and Multiple Disabilities: A Practical Guide for Every Teacher by Bob Algozzine, Jim Ysseldyke. SAGE Publications, 2006.
A must-have for teachers to help plan their curriculum as they work with children who have disabilities.

BOOKS FOR PARENTS

Children with Cerebral Palsy: A Parents' Guide edited by Elaine Geralis. Woodbine House, 1998.
A parent's guide to helping their child with cerebral palsy.

Children with Spina Bifida: A Parent's Guide edited by Marlene Lutkenhoff. Woodbine House, 1999.
A parent's guide to helping their child with spina bifida.

More than a Mom: Living a Full and Balanced Life When Your Child Has Special Needs by Amy Baskin and Heather Fawcette. Woodbine House, 2006.
Moms get lost in their children's lives. This book helps you stay yourself while balancing all the challenges you face.

Raising a Child Who Has a Physical Disability by Donna G. Albrecht. Wiley, John & Sons, Inc., 1995.
A parent's perspective is shared in an emotional and hopeful way.

Rolling Along with Goldilocks and the Three Bears by Cindy Meyers. Woodbine House, 1999.

Parents who have children with disabilities often find reading material hard to find. This is a traditional folk tale with a twist—one of the bears in a wheelchair.

WEBSITES

National Institute of Neurological Disorders and Stroke

http://www.ninds.nih.gov/

This website will answer many questions and offer support when needed. On the site search for Cerebral Palsy.

Spina Bifida Association

http://www.sbaa.org/

This site offers support for families dealing with spina bifida.

Traumatic Brain Injury

http://www.traumaticbraininjury.com/

Need questions answered? Look here.

United Cerebral Palsy Organization

http://www.ucp.org/

An advocacy site to help those dealing with the affects of cerebral palsy.

Woodbine House

http://www.woodbinehouse.com/

This is a publishin: company that specializes in special needs publications. Check it out.

GIFTED AND TALENTED

Federal definition: "'Gifted and talented', when used with respect to students, children, or youth, means students, children, or youth who give evidence of high achievement capability in areas such as intellectual, creative, artistic, or leadership capacity, or in specific academic fields, and who need services or activities not ordinarily provided by the school in order to fully develop those capabilities." [US Code, 2006,(Title IX, Part A, Section 9101(22), p. 544)]

What to look for:

Children who are gifted tend to talk early, be avid readers, are creative in problem solving, and are attentive to detail. These children look for what seem like difficult tasks to challenge their thought patterns as they seek out new knowledge. Often, they can be difficult to handle because they use such high levels of cognitive functioning. A trap to avoid is thinking that gifted children can do more work because they finish assignments early. They do not need extra homework or less time in centers. They need just the opposite. They need work that will challenge them into seeing the purpose of the assignment or center and how it will benefit them in the future.

BOOKS FOR TEACHERS

Gifted Kids' Survival Guide for Ages 10 and Under by Judy Galbraith, Pamela Espeland. Free Spirit Publishing, 1999.
This book helps kids cope with social groups, stigmas, and unrealistic teachers.

Helping Gifted Children Soar: A Practical Guide for Parents and Teachers by Carol Ann Strip, with Gretchen Hirsch. Great Potential Press, Inc., 2000.
Choosing curriculum for gifted children is always a challenging task. This books gives insight into those decisions and many others as well.

Mind Workout for Gifted Kids by Robert Allen. Barron's Educational Series, Inc., 2005.
Unlocking the mystery of giftedness.

Teaching Gifted Kids in the Regular Classroom: *Strategies and Techniques Every Teacher Can Use to Meet the Academic Needs of the Gifted and Talented* by Susan Winebrenner. Free Spirit Publishing, Inc., 2000.
Practical ideas for every classroom.

When Gifted Kids Don't Have All the Answers: How to Meet Their Social and Emotional Needs by Jim R. Delisle and Judy Galbraith. Free Spirit Publishing, Inc., 2002.
Gifted children are expected always to perform. What happens when they don't?

BOOKS FOR PARENTS

Drama of the Gifted Child: The Search for the True Self by Alice Miller. HarperCollins Publishers, 1997.
Many children who are gifted cannot find meaning in life. This book helps them and their families understand. what they have to look forward to and how talented they really are.

Parents' Guide Raising Gift Child by James Alvino. Random House Publishing Group, 1996.
Helpful tips for raising your gifted child are shared as well as ways to identify giftedness.

Survival Guide for Parents of Gifted Kids: How to Understand, Live with and Stick up for Your Gifted Child by Sally Yahnke Walker and Caryn Pernu. Free Spirit Publishing, 2002.
Just because your child is gifted does not mean that they do not come with problems. Helping you to defend your child and to ask for services.

Thinkertoys: A Handbook of Creative-Thinking Techniques by Michael Michalko. Ten Speed Press, 2006.
Helping children develop creative thinking skills.

You Know Your Child Is Gifted When . . . : A Beginner's Guide to Life on the Bright Side by Judy Galbraith. Free Spirit Publishing Inc., 2000.
A description of what to look for in your child and questions to ask, also suggests resources.

WEBSITES

American Mensa
http://www.us.mensa.org/
Designed to help gifted children reach their fullest potential.

Gifted Children
http://www.gifted-children.com/
This is a monthly newsletter designed to help parents stay on top of current research and challenges with gifted children.

Gifted Development Center
http://www.gifteddevelopment.com
What does it mean to be gifted? Look here for an answer.

NSW Assn for Gifted & Talented Children Inc.
http://www.nswagtc.org.au
Lists of characteristics to look for, as well as activities to do with your child.

National Association for Gifted Children
http://www.nagc.org/
This website is full of information from summer camps to daily lessons.

4

LESSON PLANS FOR CHILDREN WITH DISABILITIES

Children with disabilities require different plans than typically developing children. Each child will need their own individual plan to meet the goals and objectives identified in the Individualized Education Plan. Often times these lessons are written more as task analyses than the traditional lesson plan. A task analysis requires the teacher to evaluate the final skill and then break down the steps needed to reach the goal. A child then is taught skills beginning at the frustration point until the child can be successful in completing the entire task independently. An example of a task analysis is below.

TASK ANALYSIS FOR WASHING HAND

- Go to sink

- Turn on hot water

- Turn on cold water

- Put soap on your hands

- Rub hands together

- Rinse in water

- Pull down on paper towel dispenser handle

- Pull five times

- Pull paper towel off

- Dry hands

- Use paper towel and turn off hot water

- Use paper towel and turn off cold water

- Walk to trash can

- Throw away paper towel

A number of websites offer sample lesson plans for teachers. When downloading lesson plans from the Internet or another source, be sure each plan includes:

- The objective or goal of the lesson

- Materials needed

- Directions for the activity

- Appropriate age group

- Developmental appropriateness

Check the following list of websites with lesson plans and other free materials for teachers.

A to Z is a website that offers lesson plan ideas in a variety of topics from A to Z.
http://www.atozteacherstuff.com

Articles for Educators is a free resource with lessons and field trip ides.
http://www.articlesforeducators.com

Awesome Library provides links to lessons, materials, and audio visual materials. Some are for purchase and some are free.
http://www.awesomelibrary.org

Children's Lit helps teachers expand children's books to enhance the learning process.
http://www.childrenslit.com

Hoagies Gifted Education is full of links to other websites for lesson plan ideas as well as answers frequently asked questions.
http://www.hoagiesgifted.org

KinderArt is a great resource for art related lessons for children and adults of all abilities.
http://www.kinderart.com

NICHCY offers a wealth of resources for general and special educators on a variety of topics.
http://www.nichcy.org

CHAPTER

5

BOOKS FOR CHILDREN

Reading aloud is a wonderful gift that you can give to children. Through sharing an interesting book, you introduce them to a world they might not otherwise be able to visit. You can travel anywhere you like; you can have experiences that are outside the realm of your current environment; you can participate in wonderful fantasies; you can be saddened, then uplifted.

Children's desire to read and the ability to do so is fostered through being read to from the time they are born. Even babies can enjoy looking at picture books and hearing simple stories. Preschoolers love to have favorite books read to them over and over again. As children move into the school years, they can sustain their interest in books that are longer and are divided into chapters. When they realize the joy that comes from good books, they are more motivated to read on their own.

Many textbooks provide suggestions for setting up reading corners and providing books for children to read by themselves. This section will focus on books that you can read aloud to children in both small and large groups. Remember that the more you read, the better you will become at doing so. When the books have been enjoyed in a group setting, add them to the book corner for children to read alone. In addition, teachers often create lending arrangements in which children can take books home for their parents to read and then return. Teachers who believe in the importance of reading choose the best of children's literature and involve families in reading.

How to get children to listen and want more:

■ Schedule a time each day for reading. This might be toward the end of the day when children are tired and will enjoy the lack of physical activity. Make sure the setting is comfortable.

- Choose books that you enjoy, perhaps one you read as a child. Preview the book before presenting it to the children. You may find passages that you will want to shorten.

- The first time you read a book, state the title and author. Research some interesting facts about the author and share them with the children. If there is an illustrator, include that information as well.

- If you are reading to a large group, position yourself so that you are slightly higher than the children. In this way, your voice will project more easily.

- If you are reading to a small group, sit among them in a more intimate placement. This will draw them to you and to the book.

- Occasionally stop and ask, "What do you think is going to happen next?"

- Read at a pace that will allow children to build mental images of the characters or setting. Change your pace to coincide with the action of the story. Slow your pace and lower you voice during a suspenseful section. Speed it up a little when the action is moving quickly.

- Allow time for discussion only if children wish to do so. Let them voice fears, ask questions, or share their thoughts about the book. Do not turn it into a quiz or a requirement to interpret the story.

- Practice reading aloud, varying your facial expression or your tone of voice.

- Create a display containing images or information pertaining to the book you are reading. A map will allow children to pinpoint places mentioned in the story. Pictures, charts, or time lines will also add to the display. Images of or actual objects or foods mentioned in the book add another dimension.

- Find a stopping place each day that will create some suspense. You want the children to be eager to get back to the book the next day.

- When you pick up the book the next day, ask if they remember what had happened just before you stopped reading.

What Not To Do:

- Don't read a book that you do not enjoy; your feelings will be sensed by the children.

- Don't choose a book that some of the children are already familiar with. They may have heard it at home or seen a version on television or at the movies.

- Don't start a book unless you have enough time to read more than a few pages.

- Don't be fooled by awards. Just because a book has received a national book award does not mean that it is suitable for your particular group of children.

- Don't impose your own interpretations of or reactions to the story on the children. Let them express their own understanding and feelings.

CHAPTER

6

DEVELOPMENTALLY APPROPRIATE PRACTICE

NAEYC's revised position statement on Developmentally Appropriate Practice had three main motivations:

- The process of accrediting centers required widely accepted and specific definitions of what constituted excellent practices in early childhood education.

- There was a proliferation of programs that had inappropriate practices and expectations for their children, largely based on premature academic learning.

- Classrooms need to address each child's individual culture and enhance development in that culture.

The original position statement enhanced the early childhood profession, but it was not received with universal acceptance, so a revised position statement clarified some of the previous misunderstandings and expanded the vision of good practices.

It is important to keep the principles firmly in mind when making professional decisions. It is also important to use the statement in conversations with others regarding appropriate practices. Colleagues, administrators, and family members all have their individual understandings of what to do with young children. It is therefore useful for every teacher to have a copy of the position statement. In a conversation, the position statement can become a resource that eliminates the idea of personal opinions but has the weight of the professional body of knowledge. The complete statement, *Developmentally Appropriate Practice in Early Childhood Programs, Revised Edition* (1997, NAEYC), follows:

DEVELOPMENTALLY APPROPRIATE PRACTICE IN EARLY CHILDHOOD PROGRAMS SERVING CHILDREN FROM BIRTH THROUGH AGE 8

A *position statement* of the National Association for the Education of Young Children

Adopted July 1996

This statement defines and describes principles of developmentally appropriate practice in early childhood programs for administrators, teachers, parents, policy-makers, and others who make decisions about the care and education of young children. An early childhood program is any group program in a center, school, or other facility that serves children from birth through age 8. Early childhood programs include child care centers, family child care homes, private and public preschools, kinder-gartens, and primary-grade schools.

The early childhood profession is responsible for establishing and promoting standards of high-quality, professional practice in early childhood programs. These standards must reflect current knowledge and shared beliefs about what constitutes high-quality, developmentally appropriate early childhood education in the context within which services are delivered.

This position paper is organized into several components, which include the following:

1. a description of the current context in which early childhood programs operate;

2. a description of the rationale and need for NAEYC's position statement;

3. a statement of NAEYC's commitment to children;

4. the statement of the position and definition of *developmentally appropriate practice*;

5. a summary of the principles of child development and learning and the theoretical perspectives that inform decisions about early childhood practice;

6. guidelines for making decisions about developmentally appropriate practices that address the following integrated

components of early childhood practice: creating a caring community of learners, teaching to enhance children's learning and development, constructing appropriate curriculum, assessing children's learning and development, and establishing reciprocal relationships with families;

7. a challenge to the field to move from *either/or* to *both/and* thinking; and

8. recommendations for policies necessary to ensure developmentally appropriate practices for all children.

This statement is designed to be used in conjunction with NAEYC's "Criteria for High Quality Early Childhood Programs," the standards for accreditation by the National Academy of Early Childhood Programs (NAEYC 1991), and with "Guidelines for Appropriate Curriculum Content and Assessment in Programs Serving Children Ages 3 through 8" (NAEYC & NAECS/SDE 1992; Bredekamp & Rosegrant 1992, 1995).

The current context of early childhood programs

The early childhood knowledge base has expanded considerably in recent years, affirming some of the profession's cherished beliefs about good practice and challenging others. In addition to gaining new knowledge, early childhood programs have experienced several important changes in recent years. The number of programs continues to increase not only in response to the growing demand for out-of-home child care but also in recognition of the critical importance of educational experiences during the early years (Willer et al. 1991; NCES 1993). For example, in the late 1980s Head Start embarked on the largest expansion in its history, continuing this expansion into the 1990s with significant new services for families with infants and toddlers. The National Education Goals Panel established as an objective of Goal 1 that by the year 2000 all children will have access to high-quality, developmentally appropriate preschool programs (NEGP 1991). Welfare reform portends a greatly increased demand for child care services for even the youngest children from very-low-income families.

Some characteristics of early childhood programs have also changed in recent years. Increasingly, programs serve children and families from diverse cultural and linguistic backgrounds, requiring that all programs demonstrate understanding of and responsiveness to cultural and linguistic diversity. Because culture and language are critical components of children's development, practices cannot be developmentally appropriate unless they are responsive to cultural and linguistic diversity.

The Americans with Disabilities Act and the Individuals with Disabilities Education Act now require that all early childhood programs make reasonable accommodations to provide access for children with disabilities or developmental delays (DEC/CEC & NAEYC 1993). This legal right reflects the growing consensus that young children with disabilities are best served in the same community settings where their typically developing peers are found (DEC/CEC 1994).

The trend toward full inclusion of children with disabilities must be reflected in descriptions of recommended practices, and considerable work has been done toward converging the perspectives of early childhood and early childhood special education (Carta et al. 1991; Mallory 1992, 1994; Wolery, Strain, & Bailey 1992; Bredekamp 1993b; DEC Task Force 1993; Mallory & New 1994b; Wolery & Wilbers 1994).

Other important program characteristics include age of children and length of program day. Children are now enrolled in programs at younger ages, many from infancy. The length of the program day for all ages of children has been extended in response to the need for extended hours of care for employed families. Similarly, program sponsorship has become more diverse. The public schools in the majority of states now provide prekindergarten programs, some for children as young as 3, and many offer before- and after-school child care (Mitchell, Seligson, & Marx 1989; Seppanen, Kaplan deVries, & Seligson 1993; Adams & Sandfort 1994).

Corporate America has become a more visible sponsor of child care programs, with several key corporations leading the way in promoting high quality (for example, IBM, AT&T, and the American Business Collaboration). Family child care homes have become an increasingly visible sector of the child care community, with greater emphasis on professional development and the National Association for Family Child Care taking the lead in establishing an accreditation system for high-quality family child care (Hollestelle 1993; Cohen & Modigliani 1994; Galinsky et al. 1994). Many different settings in this country provide services to young children, and it is legitimate—even beneficial—for these settings to vary in certain ways. However, since it is vital to meet children's learning and developmental needs wherever they are served, high standards of quality should apply to all settings.

The context in which early childhood programs operate today is also characterized by ongoing debates about how best to teach young children and discussions about what sort of practice is most likely to contribute to their development and learning. Perhaps the most important contribution of NAEYC's 1987 position statement on developmentally appropriate practice (Bredekamp 1987) was that it created an opportunity for increased conversation within and outside the early childhood field about practices. In revising the position statement, NAEYC's goal is not only to improve the quality of current early childhood practice but also to continue to encourage the kind of questioning and debate among early childhood professionals that are necessary for the continued growth of professional knowledge in the field. A related goal is to express NAEYC's position more clearly so that energy is not wasted in unproductive debate about apparent rather than real differences of opinion.

Rationale for the position statement

The increased demand for early childhood education services is partly due to the increased recognition of the crucial importance of experiences during the earliest years of life. Children's experiences during early childhood not only influence their later functioning in school but can have effects throughout life. For example, current research demonstrates the early and lasting effects of children's environments and experiences on brain development and cognition (Chugani, Phelps, & Mazziotta 1987; Caine & Caine 1991; Kuhl 1994). Studies show that, "From infancy through about age 10, brain cells not only form most of the connections they will maintain throughout life but during this time they retain their greatest malleability" (Dana Alliance for Brain Initiatives 1996, 7).

Positive, supportive relationships, important during the earliest years of life, appear essential not only for cognitive development but also for healthy emotional development and social attachment (Bowlby 1969; Stern 1985). The preschool years are an optimum time for development of fundamental motor skills (Gallahue 1993), language development (Dyson & Genishi 1993), and other key foundational aspects of development that have life-long implications.

Recognition of the importance of the early years has heightened interest and support for early childhood education programs. A number of studies demonstrating long-term, positive consequences of participation in high-quality early childhood programs for children from low-income families influenced the expansion of Head Start and public school prekindergarten (Lazar & Darlington 1982; Lee, Brooks-Gunn, & Schuur 1988; Schweinhart, Barnes, & Weikart 1993; Campbell & Ramey 1995). Several decades of research clearly demonstrate that high-quality, developmentally appropriate early childhood programs produce short- and long-term positive effects on children's cognitive and social development (Barnett 1995).

From a thorough review of the research on the long-term effects of early childhood education programs, Barnett concludes that "across all studies, the findings were relatively uniform and constitute overwhelming evidence that early childhood care and education can produce sizeable improvements in school success" (1995, 40). Children from low-income families who participated in high-quality preschool programs were significantly less likely to have been assigned to special education, retained in grade, engaged in crime, or to have dropped out of school. The longitudinal studies, in general, suggest positive consequences for programs that used an approach consistent with principles of developmentally appropriate practice (Lazar & Darlington 1982; Berreuta-Clement et al. 1984; Miller & Bizzell 1984; Schweinhart, Weikart, & Larner 1986; Schweinhart, Barnes, & Weikart 1993; Frede 1995; Schweinhart & Weikart 1996).

Research on the long-term effects of early childhood programs indicates that children who attend good-quality child care programs, even at very young ages, demonstrate positive outcomes, and children who attend poor-quality programs show negative effects (Vandell & Powers 1983; Phillips, McCartney, & Scarr 1987; Fields et al. 1988; Vandell, Henderson, & Wilson 1988; Arnett 1989; Vandell & Corasanti 1990; Burchinal et al. 1996).

Specifically, children who experience high-quality, stable child care engage in more complex play, demonstrate more secure attachments to adults and other children, and score higher on measures of thinking ability and language development. High-quality child care can predict academic success, adjustment to school, and reduced behavioral problems for children in first grade (Howes 1988).

While the potential positive effects of high-quality child care are well documented, several large-scale evaluations of child care find that high-quality experiences are not the norm (Whitebook, Howes, & Phillips 1989; Howes, Phillips, & Whitebook 1992; Layzer, Goodson, & Moss 1993; Galinsky et al. 1994; Cost, Quality, & Child Outcomes Study Team 1995). Each of these studies, which included observations of child care and preschool quality in several states, found that good quality that supports children's health and social and cognitive development is being provided in only about 15% of programs.

Of even greater concern was the large percentage of classrooms and family child care homes that were rated "barely adequate" or "inadequate" for quality. From 12 to 20% of the children were in settings that were considered dangerous to their health and safety and harmful to their social and cognitive development. An alarming number of infants and toddlers (35 to 40%) were found to be in unsafe settings (Cost, Quality, & Child Outcomes Study Team 1995).

Experiences during the earliest years of formal schooling are also formative. Studies demonstrate that children's success or failure during the first years of school often predicts the course of later schooling (Alexander & Entwisle 1988; Slavin, Karweit, & Madden 1989). A growing body of research indicates that more developmentally appropriate teaching in preschool and kindergarten predicts greater success in the early grades (Frede & Barnett 1992; Marcon 1992; Charlesworth et al. 1993).

As with preschool and child care, the observed quality of children's early schooling is uneven (Durkin 1987, 1990; Hiebert & Papierz 1990; Bryant, Clifford, & Peisner 1991; Carnegie Task Force 1996). For instance, in a statewide observational study of kindergarten classrooms, Durkin (1987) found that despite assessment results indicating considerable individual variation in children's literacy skills, which would call for various teaching strategies as well as individual and small-group work, teachers relied on one instructional strategy—whole-group, phonics instruction—and judged children who did not learn well with this one method as unready for first grade. Currently, too many children—especially children from low-income families and some minority groups—experience school failure, are retained in grade, get assigned to special education, and eventually drop out of school (Natriello, McDill, & Pallas 1990; Legters & Slavin 1992).

Results such as these indicate that while early childhood programs have the potential for producing positive and lasting effects on children, this potential will not be achieved unless more attention is paid to ensuring that all programs meet the highest standards of quality. As the number and type of early childhood programs increase, the need increases for a shared vision and agreed-upon standards of professional practice.

NAEYC's commitment to children

It is important to acknowledge at the outset the core values that undergird all of NAEYC's work. As stated in NAEYC's *Code of Ethical Conduct*, standards of professional practice in early childhood programs are based on commitment to certain fundamental values that are deeply rooted in the history of the early childhood field:

- appreciating childhood as a unique and valuable stage of the human life cycle [and valuing the quality of children's lives in the present, not just as preparation for the future];

- basing our work with children on knowledge of child development [and learning];

- appreciating and supporting the close ties between the child and family;

- recognizing that children are best understood in the context of family, culture, and society;

- respecting the dignity, worth, and uniqueness of each individual (child, family member, and colleague); and

- helping children and adults achieve their full potential in the context of relationships that are based on trust, respect, and positive regard. (Feeney & Kipnis 1992, 3)

Statement of the position

Based on an enduring commitment to act on behalf of children, NAEYC's mission is to promote high-quality, developmentally appropriate programs for all children and their families. Because we define developmentally appropriate programs as programs that contribute to children's development, we must articulate our goals for children's development. The principles of practice advocated in this position statement are based on a set of goals for children: what we want for them, both in their present lives and as they develop to adulthood, and what personal characteristics should be fostered because these contribute to a peaceful, prosperous, and democratic society.

As we approach the 21st century, enormous changes are taking place in daily life and work. At the same time, certain human capacities will undoubtedly remain important elements in individual and societal well-being—no matter what economic or technological changes take place. With a recognition of both the continuities in human existence and the rapid changes in our world, broad agreement is emerging (e.g., Resnick 1996) that when today's children become adults they will need the ability to

- communicate well, respect others and engage with them to work through differences of opinion, and function well as members of a team;

- analyze situations, make reasoned judgments, and solve new problems as they emerge;

- access information through various modes, including spoken and written language, and intelligently employ complex tools and technologies as they are developed; and

- continue to learn new approaches, skills, and knowledge as conditions and needs change.

Clearly, people in the decades ahead will need, more than ever, fully developed literacy and numeracy skills, and these abilities are key goals of the educational process. In science, social studies (which includes history and geography), music and the visual arts, physical education and health, children need to acquire a body of knowledge and skills, as identified by those in the various disciplines (e.g., Bredekamp & Rosegrant 1995).

Besides acquiring a body of knowledge and skills, children must develop positive dispositions and attitudes. They need to understand that effort is necessary for achievement, for example, and they need to have curiosity and confidence in themselves as learners. Moreover, to live in a highly pluralistic society and world, young people need to develop a positive self-identity and a tolerance for others whose perspective and experience may be different from their own.

Beyond the shared goals of the early childhood field, every program for young children should establish its own goals in collaboration with families. All early childhood programs will not have identical goals; priorities may vary in some respects because programs serve a diversity of children and families. Such differences notwithstanding, NAEYC believes that all high-quality, developmentally appropriate programs will have certain attributes in common. A high-quality early childhood program is one that provides a safe and nurturing environment that promotes the physical, social, emotional, aesthetic, intellectual, and language development of each child while being sensitive to the needs and preferences of families.

Many factors influence the quality of an early childhood program, including (but not limited to) the extent to which knowledge about how children develop and learn is applied in program practices. Developmentally appropriate programs are based on what is known about how children develop and learn; such programs promote the development and enhance the learning of each individual child served.

Developmentally appropriate practices result from the process of professionals making decisions about the well-being and education of children based on at least three important kinds of information or knowledge:

1. *what is known about child development and learning*—knowledge of age-related human characteristics that permits general predictions within an age range about what activities, materials, interactions, or experiences will be safe, healthy, interesting, achievable, and also challenging to children;

2. *what is known about the strengths, interests, and needs of each individual child in the group* to be able to adapt for and be responsive to inevitable individual variation; and

3. *knowledge of the social and cultural contexts in which children live* to ensure that learning experiences are meaningful, relevant, and respectful for the participating children and their families.

Furthermore, each of these dimensions of knowledge—human development and learning, individual characteristics and experiences, and social and cultural contexts—is dynamic and changing, requiring that early childhood teachers remain learners throughout their careers.

An example illustrates the interrelatedness of these three dimensions of the decisionmaking process. Children all over the world acquire language at approximately the same period of the life span and in similar ways (Fernald 1992). But tremendous individual variation exists in the rate and pattern of language acquisition (Fenson et al. 1994). Also, children acquire the language or languages of the culture in which they live (Kuhl 1994). Thus, to adequately support a developmental task such as language acquisition, the teacher must draw on at least all three interrelated dimensions of knowledge to determine a developmentally appropriate strategy or intervention.

Principles of child development and learning that inform developmentally appropriate practice

Taken together, these core values define NAEYC's basic commitment to children and underlie its position on developmentally appropriate practice.

Developmentally appropriate practice is based on knowledge about how children develop and learn. As Katz states, "In a developmental approach to curriculum design, . . . [decisions] about what should be learned and how it would best be learned depend on what we know of the learner's developmental status and our understanding of the relationships between early experience and subsequent development" (1995, 109). To guide their decisions about practice, all early childhood teachers need to understand the developmental changes that typically occur in the years from birth through age 8 and beyond, variations in development that may occur, and how best to support children's learning and development during these years.

A complete discussion of the knowledge base that informs early childhood practice is beyond the scope of this document (see, for example, Seefeldt 1992; Sroufe, Cooper, & DeHart 1992; Kostelnik, Soderman, & Whiren 1993; Spodek 1993; Berk 1996). Because development and learning are so complex, no one theory is sufficient to explain these phenomena. However, a broad-based review of the literature on early childhood education generates a set of principles to inform early childhood practice. *Principles* are generalizations that are sufficiently reliable that they should be taken into account when making decisions (Katz & Chard 1989; Katz 1995). Following is a list of empirically based principles of child development and learning that inform and guide decisions about developmentally appropriate practice.

1. **Domains of children's development—physical, social, emotional, and cognitive—are closely related. Development in one domain influences and is influenced by development in other domains.**

Development in one domain can limit or facilitate development in others (Sroufe, Cooper, & DeHart 1992; Kostelnik, Soderman, & Whiren 1993). For example, when babies begin to crawl or walk, their ability to explore the world expands, and their mobility, in turn, affects their cognitive development. Likewise, children's language skill affects their ability to establish social relationships with adults and other children, just as their skill in social interaction can support or impede their language development.

Because developmental domains are interrelated, educators should be aware of and use these interrelationships to organize children's learning experiences in ways that help children develop optimally in all areas and that make meaningful connections across domains.

Recognition of the connections across developmental domains is also useful for curriculum planning with the various age groups represented in the early childhood period. Curriculum with infants and toddlers is almost solely driven by the need to support their healthy development in all domains. During the primary grades, curriculum planning attempts to help children develop conceptual understandings that apply across related subject-matter disciplines.

2. **Development occurs in a relatively orderly sequence, with later abilities, skills, and knowledge building on those already acquired.**

Human development research indicates that relatively stable, predictable sequences of growth and change occur in children during the first nine years of life (Piaget 1952; Erikson 1963; Dyson & Genishi 1993; Gallahue 1993; Case & Okamoto 1996). Predictable changes occur in all domains of development—physical, emotional, social, language, and cognitive—although the ways that these changes are manifest and the meaning attached to them may vary in different cultural contexts. Knowledge of typical development of children within the age span served by the program provides a general framework to guide how teachers prepare the learning environment and plan realistic curriculum goals and objectives and appropriate experiences.

3. **Development proceeds at varying rates from child to child as well as unevenly within different areas of each child's functioning.**

Individual variation has at least two dimensions: the inevitable variability around the average or normative course of development and the uniqueness of each person as an individual (Sroufe, Cooper, & DeHart 1992). Each child is a unique person with an individual pattern and timing of growth, as well as individual personality, temperament, learning style, and experiential and family background. All children have their own strengths, needs, and interests; for some children, special learning and developmental needs or abilities are identified. Given the enormous variation among children of the same chronological age, a child's age must be recognized as only a crude index of developmental maturity.

Recognition that individual variation is not only to be expected but also valued requires that decisions about curriculum and adults' interactions with children be as individualized as possible. Emphasis on individual appropriateness is not the same as "individualism." Rather, this recognition requires that children be considered not solely as members of an age group, expected to perform to a predetermined norm and without adaptation to individual variation of any kind. Having high expectations for all children is important, but rigid expectations of group norms do not reflect what is known about real differences in individual development and learning during the early years. Group-norm expectancy can be especially harmful for children with special learning and developmental needs (NEGP 1991; Mallory 1992; Wolery, Strain, & Bailey 1992).

4. **Early experiences have both cumulative and delayed effects on individual children's development; optimal periods exist for certain types of development and learning.**

Children's early experiences, either positive or negative, are cumulative in the sense that if an experience occurs occasionally, it may have minimal effects. If positive or negative experiences occur frequently, however, they can have powerful, lasting, even "snowballing," effects (Katz & Chard 1989; Kostelnik, Soderman, & Whiren 1993; Wieder & Greenspan 1993). For example, a child's social experiences with other children in the preschool years help him develop social skills and confidence that enable him to make friends in the early school years, and these experiences further enhance the child's social competence. Conversely, children who fail to develop minimal social competence and are neglected or rejected by peers are at significant risk to drop out of school, become delinquent, and experience mental health problems in adulthood (Asher, Hymel, & Renshaw 1984; Parker & Asher 1987).

Similar patterns can be observed in babies whose cries and other attempts at communication are regularly responded to, thus enhancing their own sense of efficacy and increasing communicative competence. Likewise, when children have or do not have early literacy experiences, such as being read to regularly, their later success in learning to read is affected accordingly. Perhaps most convincing is the growing body of research demonstrating that social and sensorimotor experiences during the first three years directly affect neurological development of the brain, with important and lasting implications for children's capacity to learn (Dana Alliance for Brain Initiatives 1996).

Early experiences can also have delayed effects, either positive or negative, on subsequent development. For instance, some evidence suggests that reliance on extrinsic rewards (such as candy or money) to shape children's behavior, a strategy that can be very effective in the short term, under certain circumstances lessens children's intrinsic motivation to engage in the rewarded behavior in the long term (Dweck 1986; Kohn 1993). For example, paying children to read books may over time undermine their desire to read for their own enjoyment and edification.

At certain points in the life span, some kinds of learning and development occur most efficiently. For example, the first three years of life appear to be an optimal period for verbal language development (Kuhl 1994). Although delays in language development due to physical or environmental deficits can be ameliorated later on, such intervention usually requires considerable effort. Similarly, the preschool years appear to be optimum for fundamental motor development (that is, fundamental motor skills are more easily and efficiently acquired at this age) (Gallahue 1995). Children who have many opportunities and adult support to practice large-motor skills (running, jumping, hopping, skipping) during this period have the cumulative benefit of being better able to acquire more sophisticated, complex motor skills (balancing on a beam or riding a two-wheel bike) in subsequent years. On the other hand, children whose early motor experiences are severely limited may struggle to acquire physical competence and may also experience delayed effects when attempting to participate in sports or personal fitness activities later in life.

5. Development proceeds in predictable directions toward greater complexity, organization, and internalization.

Learning during early childhood proceeds from behavioral knowledge to symbolic or representational knowledge (Bruner 1983). For example, children learn to navigate their homes and other familiar settings long before they can understand the words *left* and *right* or read a map of the house. Developmentally appropriate programs provide opportunities for children to broaden and deepen their behavioral knowledge by providing a variety of firsthand experiences and by helping children acquire symbolic knowledge through representing their experiences in a variety of media, such as drawing, painting, construction of models, dramatic play, verbal and written descriptions (Katz 1995).

Even very young children are able to use various media to represent their understanding of concepts. Furthermore, through representation of their knowledge, the knowledge itself is enhanced (Edwards, Gandini, & Forman 1993; Malaguzzi 1993; Forman 1994). Representational modes and media also vary with the age of the child. For instance, most learning for infants and toddlers is sensory and motoric, but by age 2 children use one object to stand for another in play (a block for a phone or a spoon for a guitar).

6. Development and learning occur in and are influenced by multiple social and cultural contexts.

Bronfenbrenner (1979, 1989, 1993) provides an ecological model for understanding human development. He explains that children's development is best understood within the sociocultural context of the family, educational setting, community, and broader society. These various contexts are interrelated, and all have an impact on the developing child. For example, even a child in a loving, supportive family within a strong, healthy community is affected by the biases of the larger society, such as racism or sexism, and may show the effects of negative stereotyping and discrimination.

We define *culture* as the customary beliefs and patterns of and for behavior, both explicit and implicit, that are passed on to future generations by the society they live in and/or by a social, religious, or ethnic group within it. Because culture is often discussed in the context of diversity or multiculturalism, people fail to recognize the powerful role that culture plays in influencing the development of *all* children. Every culture structures and interprets children's behavior and development (Edwards & Gandini 1989; Tobin, Wu, & Davidson 1989; Rogoff et al. 1993). As Bowman states, "Rules of development are the same for all children, but social contexts shape children's development into different configurations" (1994, 220). Early childhood teachers need to understand the influence of sociocultural contexts on learning, recognize children's developing competence, and accept a variety of ways for children to express their developmental achievements (Vygotsky 1978; Wertsch 1985; Forman, Minick, & Stone 1993; New 1993, 1994; Bowman & Stott 1994; Mallory & New 1994a; Phillips 1994; Bruner 1996; Wardle 1996).

Teachers should learn about the culture of the majority of the children they serve if that culture differs from their own. However, recognizing that development and learning are influenced by social and cultural contexts does not require teachers to understand all the nuances of every cultural group they may encounter in their practice; this would be an impossible task. Rather, this fundamental recognition sensitizes teachers to the need to acknowledge how their own cultural experience shapes their perspective and to realize that multiple perspectives, in addition to their own, must be considered in decisions about children's development and learning.

Children are capable of learning to function in more than one cultural context simultaneously. However, if teachers set low expectations for children based on their home culture and language, children cannot develop and learn optimally. Education should be an additive process. For example, children whose primary language is not English should be able to learn English without being forced to give up their home language (NAEYC 1996a). Likewise, children who speak only English benefit from learning another language. The goal is that all children learn to function well in the society as a whole and move comfortably among groups of people who come from both similar and dissimilar backgrounds.

7. **Children are active learners, drawing on direct physical and social experience as well as culturally transmitted knowledge to construct their own understandings of the world around them.**

Children contribute to their own development and learning as they strive to make meaning out of their daily experiences in the home, the early childhood program, and the community. Principles of developmentally appropriate practice are based on several prominent theories that view intellectual development from a constructivist, interactive perspective (Dewey 1916; Piaget 1952; Vygotsky 1978; DeVries & Kohlberg 1990; Rogoff 1990; Gardner 1991; Kamii & Ewing 1996).

From birth, children are actively engaged in constructing their own understandings from their experiences, and these understandings are mediated by and clearly linked to the sociocultural context. Young children actively learn from observing and participating with other children and adults, including parents and teachers. Children need to form their own hypotheses and keep trying them out through social interaction, physical manipulation, and their own thought processes—observing what happens, reflecting on their findings, asking questions, and formulating answers. When objects, events, and other people challenge the working model that the child has mentally constructed, the child is forced to adjust the model or alter the mental structures to account for the new information. Throughout early childhood, the child in processing new experiences continually reshapes, expands, and reorganizes mental structures (Piaget 1952; Vygotsky 1978; Case & Okamoto 1996). When teachers and other adults use various strategies to encourage children to reflect on their experiences by planning beforehand and "revisiting" afterward, the knowledge and understanding gained from the experience is deepened (Copple, Sigel, & Saunders 1984; Edwards, Gandini, & Forman 1993; Stremmel & Fu 1993; Hohmann & Weikart 1995).

In the statement of this principle, the term "physical and social experience" is used in the broadest sense to include children's exposure to physical knowledge, learned through firsthand experience of using objects (observing that a ball thrown in the air falls down), and social knowledge, including the vast body of culturally acquired and transmitted knowledge that children need to function in the world. For example, children progressively construct their own understanding of various symbols, but the symbols they use (such as the alphabet or numerical system) are the ones used within their culture and transmitted to them by adults.

In recent years, discussions of cognitive development have at times become polarized (see Seifert 1993). Piaget's theory stressed that development of certain cognitive structures was a necessary prerequisite to learning (i.e., development precedes learning), while other research has demonstrated that instruction in specific concepts or strategies can facilitate development of more mature cognitive structures (learning precedes development) (Vygotsky 1978; Gelman & Baillargeon 1983). Current attempts to resolve this apparent dichotomy (Seifert 1993; Sameroff & McDonough 1994; Case & Okamoto 1996) acknowledge that essentially both theoretical perspectives are correct in explaining aspects of cognitive development during early childhood. Strategic teaching, of course, can enhance children's learning. Yet, direct instruction may be totally ineffective; it fails when it is not attuned to the cognitive capacities and knowledge of the child at that point in development.

8. Development and learning result from interaction of biological maturation and the environment, which includes both the physical and social worlds that children live in.

The simplest way to express this principle is that human beings are products of both heredity and environment and these forces are interrelated. Behaviorists focus on the environmental influences that determine learning, while maturationists emphasize the unfolding of predetermined, hereditary characteristics. Each perspective is true to some extent, and yet neither perspective is sufficient to explain learning or development. More often today, development is viewed as the result of an interactive, transactional process between the growing, changing individual and his or her experiences in the social and physical worlds (Scarr & McCartney 1983; Plomin 1994a, b). For example, a child's genetic makeup may predict healthy growth, but inadequate nutrition in the early years of life may keep this potential from being fulfilled. Or a severe disability, whether inherited or environmentally caused, may be ameliorated through systematic, appropriate intervention. Likewise, a child's inherited temperament—whether a predisposition to be wary or outgoing—shapes and is shaped by how other children and adults communicate with that child.

9. **Play is an important vehicle for children's social, emotional, and cognitive development, as well as a reflection of their development.**

Understanding that children are active constructors of knowledge and that development and learning are the result of interactive processes, early childhood teachers recognize that children's play is a highly supportive context for these developing processes (Piaget 1952; Fein 1981; Bergen 1988; Smilansky & Shefatya 1990; Fromberg 1992; Berk & Winsler 1995). Play gives children opportunities to understand the world, interact with others in social ways, express and control emotions, and develop their symbolic capabilities. Children's play gives adults insights into children's development and opportunities to support the development of new strategies. Vygotsky (1978) believed that play leads development, with written language growing out of oral language through the vehicle of symbolic play that promotes the development of symbolic representation abilities. Play provides a context for children to practice newly acquired skills and also to function on the edge of their developing capacities to take on new social roles, attempt novel or challenging tasks, and solve complex problems that they would not (or could not) otherwise do (Mallory & New 1994b).

Research demonstrates the importance of sociodramatic play as a tool for learning curriculum content with 3- through 6-year-old children. When teachers provide a thematic organization for play; offer appropriate props, space, and time; and become involved in the play by extending and elaborating on children's ideas, children's language and literacy skills can be enhanced (Levy, Schaefer, & Phelps 1986; Schrader 1989, 1990; Morrow 1990; Pramling 1991; Levy, Wolfgang, & Koorland 1992).

In addition to supporting cognitive development, play serves important functions in children's physical, emotional, and social development (Herron & Sutton-Smith 1971). Children express and represent their ideas, thoughts, and feelings when engaged in symbolic play. During play a child can learn to deal with emotions, to interact with others, to resolve conflicts, and to gain a sense of competence—all in the safety that only play affords. Through play, children also can develop their imaginations and creativity. There-fore, child-initiated, teacher-supported play is an essential com-ponent of developmentally appropriate practice (Fein & Rivkin 1986).

10. **Development advances when children have opportunities to practice newly acquired skills as well as when they experience a challenge just beyond the level of their present mastery.**

Research demonstrates that children need to be able to successfully negotiate learning tasks most of the time if they are to maintain motivation and persistence (Lary 1990; Brophy 1992). Confronted by repeated failure, most children will simply stop trying. So most of the time, teachers should give young children tasks that with effort they can accomplish and present them with content that is accessible at their level of understanding. At the same time, chil-dren continually gravitate to situations and stimuli that give them the chance to work at their "growing edge" (Berk & Winsler 1995; Bodrova & Leong 1996). Moreover, in a task just beyond the child's independent reach, the adult and more-competent peers contrib-ute significantly to development by providing the supportive "scaf-folding" that allows the child to take the next step.

Development and learning are dynamic processes requiring that adults understand the continuum, observe children closely to match curriculum and teaching to children's emerging competencies, needs, and interests, and then help children move forward by targeting educational experiences to the edge of children's changing capacities so as to challenge but not frustrate them. Human beings, especially children, are highly motivated to understand what they almost, but not quite, comprehend and to master what they can almost, but not quite, do (White 1965; Vygotsky 1978). The principle of learning is that children can do things first in a supportive context and then later independently and in a variety of contexts. Rogoff (1990) describes the process of adult-assisted learning as "guided participation" to emphasize that children actively collaborate with others to move to more complex levels of understanding and skill.

11. **Children demonstrate different modes of knowing and learning and different ways of representing what they know.**

For some time, learning theorists and developmental psychologists have recognized that human beings come to understand the world in many ways and that individuals tend to have preferred or stronger modes of learning. Studies of differences in learning modalities have contrasted visual, auditory, or tactile learners. Other work has identified learners as field-dependent or independent (Witkin 1962). Gardner (1983) expanded on this concept by theorizing that human beings possess at least seven "intelligences." In addition to having the ones traditionally emphasized in schools, linguistic and logical-mathematical, individuals are more or less proficient in at least these other areas: musical, spatial, bodily-kinesthetic, intrapersonal, and interpersonal.

Malaguzzi (1993) used the metaphor of "100 languages" to describe the diverse modalities through which children come to understand the world and represent their knowledge. The processes of representing their understanding can with the assistance of teachers help children deepen, improve, and expand their understanding (Copple, Sigel, & Saunders 1984; Forman 1994; Katz 1995). The principle of diverse modalities implies that teachers should provide not only opportunities for individual children to use their preferred modes of learning to capitalize on their strengths (Hale-Benson 1986) but also opportunities to help children develop in the modes or intelligences in which they may not be as strong.

12. **Children develop and learn best in the context of a community where they are safe and valued, their physical needs are met, and they feel psychologically secure.**

Maslow (1954) conceptualized a hierarchy of needs in which learning was not considered possible unless physical and psychological needs for safety and security were first met. Because children's physical health and safety too often are threatened today, programs for young children must not only provide adequate health, safety, and nutrition but may also need to ensure more comprehensive services, such as physical, dental, and mental health and social services (NASBE 1991; U.S. Department of Health & Human Services 1996). In addition, children's development in all areas is influenced by their ability to establish and maintain a limited number of positive, consistent primary relationships with adults and other children (Bowlby 1969; Stern 1985; Garbarino et al. 1992). These primary relationships begin in the family but extend over time to include children's teachers and members of the community; therefore, practices that are developmentally appropriate address children's physical, social, and emotional needs as well as their intellectual development.

Guidelines for decisions about developmentally appropriate practice

A linear listing of principles of child development and learning, such as the above, cannot do justice to the complexity of the phenomena that it attempts to describe and explain. Just as all domains of development and learning are interrelated, so, too, there are relationships among the principles. Similarly, the following guidelines for practice do not match up one-to-one with the principles. Instead, early childhood professionals draw on all these fundamental ideas (as well as many others) when making decisions about their practice.

An understanding of the nature of development and learning during the early childhood years, from birth through age 8, generates guidelines that inform the practices of early childhood educators. Developmentally appropriate practice requires that teachers integrate the many dimensions of their knowledge base. They must know about child development and the implications of this knowledge for how to teach, the content of the curriculum—what to teach and when—how to assess what children have learned, and how to adapt curriculum and instruction to children's individual strengths, needs, and interests. Further, they must know the particular children they teach and their families and be knowledgeable as well about the social and cultural context.

The following guidelines address five interrelated dimensions of early childhood professional practice: creating a caring community of learners, teaching to enhance development and learning, constructing appropriate curriculum, assessing children's development and learning, and establishing reciprocal relationships with families. (The word *teacher* is used to refer to any adult responsible for a group of children in any early childhood program, including infant/toddler caregivers, family child care providers, and specialists in other disciplines who fulfill the role of teacher.)

Examples of appropriate and inappropriate practice in relation to each of these dimensions are given for infants and toddlers (Part 3, pp. 72–90), children 3 through 5 (Part 4, pp. 123–35), and children 6 through 8 (Part 5, pp. 161–78). In the references at the end of each part, readers will be able to find fuller discussion of the points summarized here and strategies for implementation.

1. Creating a caring community of learners

Developmentally appropriate practices occur within a context that supports the development of relationships between adults and children, among children, among teachers, and between teachers and families. Such a community reflects what is known about the social construction of knowledge and the importance of establishing a caring, inclusive community in which all children can develop and learn.

A. The early childhood setting functions as a community of learners in which all participants consider and contribute to each other's well-being and learning.

B. Consistent, positive relationships with a limited number of adults and other children are a fundamental determinant of healthy human development and provide the context for children to learn about themselves and their world and also how to develop positive, constructive relationships with other people. The early childhood classroom is a community in which each child is valued. Children learn to respect and acknowledge differences in abilities and talents and to value each person for his or her strengths.

C. Social relationships are an important context for learning. Each child has strengths or interests that contribute to the overall functioning of the group. When children have opportunities to play together, work on projects in small groups, and talk with other children and adults, their own development and learning are enhanced. Interacting with other children in small groups provides a context for children to operate on the edge of their developing capacities. The learning environment enables children to construct understanding through interactions with adults and other children.

D. The learning environment is designed to protect children's health and safety and is supportive of children's physiological needs for activity, sensory stimulation, fresh air, rest, and nourishment. The program provides a balance of rest and active movement for children throughout the program day. Outdoor experiences are provided for children of all ages. The program protects children's psychological safety; that is, children feel secure, relaxed, and comfortable rather than disengaged, frightened, worried, or stressed.

E. Children experience an organized environment and an orderly routine that provides an overall structure in which learning takes place; the environment is dynamic and changing but predictable and comprehensible from a child's point of view. The learning environment provides a variety of materials and opportunities for children to have firsthand, meaningful experiences.

2. Teaching to enhance development and learning

Adults are responsible for ensuring children's healthy development and learning. From birth, relationships with adults are critical determinants of children's healthy social and emotional development and serve as well as mediators of language and intellectual development. At the same time, children are active constructors of their own understanding, who benefit from initiating and regulating their own learning activities and interacting with peers. Therefore, early childhood teachers strive to achieve an optimal balance between children's self-initiated learning and adult guidance or support.

Teachers accept responsibility for actively supporting children's development and provide occasions for children to acquire important knowledge and skills. Teachers use their knowledge of child development and learning to identify the range of activities, materials, and learning experiences that are appropriate for a group or individual child. This knowledge is used in conjunction with knowledge of the context and understanding about individual children's growth patterns, strengths, needs, interests, and experiences to design the curriculum and learning environment and guide teachers' interactions with children. The following guidelines describe aspects of the teachers' role in making decisions about practice:

A. Teachers respect, value, and accept children and treat them with dignity at all times.

B. Teachers make it a priority to know each child well.

(1) Teachers establish positive, personal relationships with children to foster the child's development and keep informed about the child's needs and potentials. Teachers listen to children and adapt their responses to children's differing needs, interests, styles, and abilities.

(2) Teachers continually observe children's spontaneous play and interaction with the physical environment and with other children to learn about their interests, abilities, and developmental progress. On the basis of this information, teachers plan experiences that enhance children's learning and development.

(3) Understanding that children develop and learn in the context of their families and communities, teachers establish relationships with families that increase their knowledge of children's lives outside the classroom and their awareness of the perspectives and priorities of those individuals most significant in the child's life.

(4) Teachers are alert to signs of undue stress and traumatic events in children's lives and aware of effective strategies to reduce stress and support the development of resilience.

(5) Teachers are responsible at all times for all children under their supervision and plan for children's increasing development of self-regulation abilities.

C. Teachers create an intellectually engaging, responsive environment to promote each child's learning and development.

(1) Teachers use their knowledge about children in general and the particular children in the group as well as their familiarity with what children need to learn and develop

in each curriculum area to organize the environment and plan curriculum and teaching strategies.

(2) Teachers provide children with a rich variety of experiences, projects, materials, problems, and ideas to explore and investigate, ensuring that these are worthy of children's attention.

(3) Teachers provide children with opportunities to make meaningful choices and time to explore through active involvement. Teachers offer children the choice to participate in a small-group or a solitary activity, assist and guide children who are not yet able to use and enjoy child-choice activity periods, and provide opportunities for practice of skills as a self-chosen activity.

(4) Teachers organize the daily and weekly schedule and allocate time so as to provide children with extended blocks of time in which to engage in play, projects, and/or study in integrated curriculum.

D. Teachers make plans to enable children to attain key curriculum goals across various disciplines, such as language arts, mathematics, social studies, science, art, music, physical education, and health (see "Constructing appropriate curriculum," pp. 20–21).

(1) Teachers incorporate a wide variety of experiences, materials and equipment, and teaching strategies in constructing curriculum to accommodate a broad range of children's individual differences in prior experiences, maturation rates, styles of learning, needs, and interests.

(2) Teachers bring each child's home culture and language into the shared culture of the school so that the unique contributions of each group are recognized and valued by others.

(3) Teachers are prepared to meet identified special needs of individual children, including children with disabilities and those who exhibit unusual interests and skills. Teachers use all the strategies identified here, consult with appropriate specialists, and see that the child gets the specialized services he or she requires.

E. Teachers foster children's collaboration with peers on interesting, important enterprises.

(1) Teachers promote children's productive collaboration without taking over to the extent that children lose interest.

(2) Teachers use a variety of ways of flexibly grouping children for the purposes of instruction, supporting collaboration among children, and building a sense of community. At various times, children have opportunities to work individually, in small groups, and with the whole group.

F. Teachers develop, refine, and use a wide repertoire of teaching strategies to enhance children's learning and development.

(1) To help children develop their initiative, teachers encourage them to choose and plan their own learning activities.

(2) Teachers pose problems, ask questions, and make comments and suggestions that stimulate children's thinking and extend their learning.

(3) Teachers extend the range of children's interests and the scope of their thought through presenting novel experiences and introducing stimulating ideas, problems, experiences, or hypotheses.

(4) To sustain an individual child's effort or engagement in purposeful activities, teachers select from a range of strategies, including but not limited to modeling, demonstrating specific skills, and providing information, focused attention, physical proximity, verbal encouragement, reinforcement and other behavioral procedures, as well as additional structure and modification of equipment or schedules as needed.

(5) Teachers coach and/or directly guide children in the acquisition of specific skills as needed.

(6) Teachers calibrate the complexity and challenge of activities to suit children's level of skill and knowledge, increasing the challenge as children gain competence and understanding.

(7) Teachers provide cues and other forms of "scaffolding" that enable the child to succeed in a task that is just beyond his or her ability to complete alone.

(8) To strengthen children's sense of competence and confidence as learners, motivation to persist, and willingness to take risks, teachers provide experiences for children to be genuinely successful and to be challenged.

(9) To enhance children's conceptual understanding, teachers use various strategies that encourage children to reflect on and "revisit" their learning experiences.

G. Teachers facilitate the development of responsibility and self-regulation in children.

(1) Teachers set clear, consistent, and fair limits for children's behavior and hold children accountable to standards of acceptable behavior. To the extent that children are able, teachers engage them in developing rules and procedures for behavior of class members.

(2) Teachers redirect children to more acceptable behavior or activity or use children's mistakes as learning opportunities, patiently reminding children of rules and their rationale as needed.

(3) Teachers listen and acknowledge children's feelings and frustrations, respond with respect, guide children to resolve conflicts, and model skills that help children to solve their own problems.

3. Constructing appropriate curriculum

The content of the early childhood curriculum is determined by many factors, including the subject matter of the disciplines, social or cultural values, and parental input. In developmentally appropriate programs, decisions about curriculum content also take into consideration the age and experience of the learners. Achieving success for all children depends, among other essentials, on providing a challenging, interesting, developmentally appropriate curriculum. NAEYC does not endorse specific curricula. However, one purpose of these guidelines is as a framework for making decisions about developing curriculum or selecting a curriculum model. Teachers who use a validated curriculum model benefit from the evidence of its effectiveness and the accumulated wisdom and experience of others.

In some respects, the curriculum strategies of many teachers today do not demand enough of children and in other ways demand too much of the wrong thing. On the one hand, narrowing the curriculum to those basic skills that can be easily measured on multiple-choice tests diminishes the intellectual challenge for many children. Such intellectually impoverished curriculum underestimates the true competence of children, which has been demonstrated to be much higher than is often assumed (Gelman & Baillargeon 1983; Gelman & Meck 1983; Edwards, Gandini, & Forman 1993; Resnick 1996). Watereddown, oversimplified curriculum leaves many children unchallenged, bored, uninterested, or unmotivated. In such situations, children's experiences are marked by a great many missed opportunities for learning.

On the other hand, curriculum expectations in the early years of schooling sometimes are not appropriate for the age groups served. When next-grade expectations of mastery of basic skills are routinely pushed down to the previous grade and whole group and teacher-led instruction is the dominant teaching strategy, children who cannot sit still and attend to teacher lectures or who are bored and unchallenged or frustrated by doing workbook pages for long periods of time are mislabeled as immature, disruptive, or unready for school (Shepard & Smith 1988). Constructing appropriate curriculum requires attention to at least the following guidelines for practice:

A. Developmentally appropriate curriculum provides for all areas of a child's development: physical, emotional, social, linguistic, aesthetic, and cognitive.

B. Curriculum includes a broad range of content across disciplines that is socially relevant, intellectually engaging, and personally meaningful to children.

C. Curriculum builds upon what children already know and are able to do (activating prior knowledge) to consolidate their learning and to foster their acquisition of new concepts and skills.

D. Effective curriculum plans frequently integrate across traditional subject-matter divisions to help children make meaningful connections and provide opportunities for rich conceptual development; focusing on one subject is also a valid strategy at times.

E. Curriculum promotes the development of knowledge and understanding, processes and skills, as well as the dispositions to use and apply skills and to go on learning.

F. Curriculum content has intellectual integrity, reflecting the key concepts and tools of inquiry of recognized disciplines in ways that are accessible and achievable for young children, ages 3 through 8 (e.g., Bredekamp & Rosegrant 1992, 1995). Children directly participate in study of the disciplines, for instance, by conducting scientific experiments, writing, performing, solving mathematical problems, collecting and analyzing data, collecting oral history, and performing other roles of experts in the disciplines.

G. Curriculum provides opportunities to support children's home culture and language while also developing all children's abilities to participate in the shared culture of the program and the community.

H. Curriculum goals are realistic and attainable for most children in the designated age range for which they are designed.

I. When used, technology is physically and philosophically integrated in the classroom curriculum and teaching. (See "NAEYC Position Statement: Technology and Young Children—Ages Three through Eight" [NAEYC 1996b].)

4. Assessing children's learning and development

Assessment of individual children's development and learning is essential for planning and implementing appropriate curriculum. In developmentally appropriate programs, assessment and curriculum are integrated, with teachers continually engaging in observational assessment for the purpose of improving teaching and learning.

Accurate assessment of young children is difficult because their development and learning are rapid, uneven, episodic, and embedded within specific cultural and linguistic contexts. Too often, inaccurate and inappropriate assessment measures have been used to label, track, or otherwise harm young children. Developmentally appropriate assessment practices are based on the following guidelines:

A. Assessment of young children's progress and achievements is ongoing, strategic, and purposeful. The results of assessment are used to benefit children—in adapting curriculum and teaching to meet the developmental and learning needs of children, communicating with the child's family, and evaluating the program's effectiveness for the purpose of improving the program.

B. The content of assessments reflects progress toward important learning and developmental goals. The program has a systematic plan for collecting and using assessment information that is integrated with curriculum planning.

C. The methods of assessment are appropriate to the age and experiences of young children. Therefore, assessment of young children relies heavily on the results of observations of children's development, descriptive data, collections of representative work by children, and demonstrated performance during authentic, not contrived, activities. Input from families as well as children's evaluations of their own work are part of the overall assessment strategy.

D. Assessments are tailored to a specific purpose and used only for the purpose for which they have been demonstrated to produce reliable, valid information.

E. Decisions that have a major impact on children, such as enrollment or placement, are never made on the basis of a single developmental assessment or screening device but are based on multiple sources of relevant information, particularly observations by teachers and parents.

F. To identify children who have special learning or developmental needs and to plan appropriate curriculum and teaching for them, developmental assessments and observations are used.

G. Assessment recognizes individual variation in learners and allows for differences in styles and rates of learning. Assessment takes into consideration such factors as the child's facility in English, stage of language acquisition, and whether the child has had the time and opportunity to develop proficiency in his or her home language as well as in English.

H. Assessment legitimately addresses not only what children can do independently but what they can do with assistance from other children or adults. Teachers study children as individuals as well as in relationship to groups by documenting group projects and other collaborative work. (For a more complete discussion of principles of appropriate assessment, see the position statement *Guidelines for Appropriate Curriculum Content and Assessment for Children Ages 3 through 8* [NAEYC & NAECS/SDE 1992]; see also Shepard 1994.)

5. Establishing reciprocal relationships with families

Developmentally appropriate practices derive from deep knowledge of individual children and the context within which they develop and learn. The younger the child, the more necessary it is for professionals to acquire this knowledge through relationships with children's families. The traditional approach to families has been a parent education orientation in which the professionals see themselves as knowing what is best for children and view parents as needing to be educated. There is also the limited view of parent involvement that sees PTA membership as the primary goal. These approaches do not adequately convey the complexity of the partnership between teachers and parents that is a fundamental element of good practice (Powell 1994).

When the parent education approach is criticized in favor of a more family-centered approach, this shift may be misunderstood to mean that parents dictate all program content and professionals abdicate responsibility, doing whatever parents want regardless of whether professionals agree that it is in children's best interest. Either of these extremes oversimplifies the importance of relationships with families and fails to provide the kind of environment in which parents and professionals work together to achieve shared goals for children; such programs with this focus are characterized by at least the following guidelines for practice:

A. Reciprocal relationships between teachers and families require mutual respect, cooperation, shared responsibility, and negotiation of conflicts toward achievement of shared goals.

B. Early childhood teachers work in collaborative partnerships with families, establishing and maintaining regular, frequent two-way communication with children's parents.

C. Parents are welcome in the program and participate in decisions about their children's care and education. Parents observe and participate and serve in decisionmaking roles in the program.

D. Teachers acknowledge parents' choices and goals for children and respond with sensitivity and respect to parents' preferences and concerns without abdicating professional responsibility to children.

E. Teachers and parents share their knowledge of the child and understanding of children's development and learning as part of day-to-day communication and planned conferences. Teachers support families in ways that maximally promote family decisionmaking capabilities and competence.

F. To ensure more accurate and complete information, the program involves families in assessing and planning for individual children.

G. The program links families with a range of services, based on identified resources, priorities, and concerns.

H. Teachers, parents, programs, social service and health agencies, and consultants who may have educational responsibility for the child at different times should, with family participation, share developmental information about children as they pass from one level or program to another.

Moving from either/or to both/and thinking in early childhood practice

Some critical reactions to NAEYC's (1987) position statement on developmentally appropriate practice reflect a recurring tendency in the American discourse on education: the polarizing into *either/or* choices of many questions that are more fruitfully seen as *both/ands*. For example, heated debates have broken out about whether children in the early grades should receive wholelanguage or phonics instruction, when, in fact, the two approaches are quite compatible and most effective in combination.

It is true that there are practices that are clearly inappropriate for early childhood professionals—use of physical punishment or disparaging verbal comments about children, discriminating against children or their families, and many other examples that could be cited (see Parts 3, 4, and 5 for examples relevant to different age groups). However, most questions about practice require more complex responses. It is not that children need food **or** water; they need both.

To illustrate the many ways that early childhood practice draws on *both/and* thinking and to convey some of the complexity and interrelationship among the principles that guide our practice, we offer the following statements as **examples**:

- Children construct their own understanding of concepts, **and** they benefit from instruction by more competent peers and adults.

- Children benefit from opportunities to see connections across disciplines through integration of curriculum **and** from opportunities to engage in in-depth study within a content area.

- Children benefit from predictable structure and orderly routine in the learning environment **and** from the teacher's flexibility and spontaneity in responding to their emerging ideas, needs, and interests.

- Children benefit from opportunities to make meaningful choices about what they will do and learn **and** from having a clear understanding of the boundaries within which choices are permissible.

- Children benefit from situations that challenge them to work at the edge of their developing capacities **and** from ample opportunities to practice newly acquired skills and to acquire the disposition to persist.

- Children benefit from opportunities to collaborate with their peers and acquire a sense of being part of a community **and** from being treated as individuals with their own strengths, interests, and needs.

- Children need to develop a positive sense of their own self-identity **and** respect for other people whose perspectives and experiences may be different from their own.

- Children have enormous capacities to learn and almost boundless curiosity about the world, **and** they have recognized, age-related limits on their cognitive and linguistic capacities.

- Children benefit from engaging in self-initiated, spontaneous play **and** from teacher-planned and -structured activities, projects, and experiences.

The above list is not exhaustive. Many more examples could be cited to convey the interrelationships among the principles of child development and learning or among the guidelines for early childhood practice.

Policies essential for achieving developmentally appropriate early childhood programs

Early childhood professionals working in diverse situations with varying levels of funding and resources are responsible for implementing practices that are developmentally appropriate for the children they serve. Regardless of the resources available, professionals have an ethical responsibility to practice, to the best of their ability, according to the standards of their profession. Nevertheless, the kinds of practices advocated in this position statement are more likely to be implemented within an infrastructure of supportive policies and resources. NAEYC strongly recommends that policymaking groups at the state and local levels consider the following when implementing early childhood programs:

1. A comprehensive professional preparation and development system is in place to ensure that early childhood programs are staffed with qualified personnel (NAEYC 1994).

    ■ A system exists for early childhood professionals to acquire the knowledge and practical skills needed to practice through collegelevel specialized preparation in early childhood education/child development.

    ■ Teachers in early childhood programs are encouraged and supported to obtain and maintain, through study and participation in inservice training, current knowledge of child development and learning and its application to early childhood practice.

    ■ Specialists in early childhood special education are available to provide assistance and consultation in meeting the individual needs of children in the program.

    ■ In addition to management and supervision skills, administrators of early childhood programs have appropriate professional qualifications, including training specific to the education and development of young children, and they provide teachers time and opportunities to work collaboratively with colleagues and parents.

2. Funding is provided to ensure adequate staffing of early childhood programs and fair staff compensation that promotes continuity of relationships among adults and children (Willer 1990).

- Funding is adequate to limit the size of the groups and provide sufficient numbers of adults to ensure individualized and appropriate care and education. Even the most well-qualified teacher cannot individualize instruction and adequately supervise too large a group of young children. An acceptable adult-child ratio for 4- and 5-year-olds is two adults with no more than 20 children (Ruopp et al. 1979; Francis & Self 1982; Howes 1983; Taylor & Taylor 1989; Howes, Phillips, & Whitebook 1992; Cost, Quality, & Child Outcomes Study Team 1995; Howes, Smith, & Galinsky 1995). Younger children require much smaller groups. Group size and ratio of children to adults should increase gradually through the primary grades, but one teacher with no more than 18 children or two adults with no more than 25 children is optimum (Nye et al. 1992; Nye, Boyd-Zaharias, & Fulton 1994). Inclusion of children with disabilities may necessitate additional adults or smaller group size to ensure that all children's needs are met.

- Programs offer staff salaries and benefits commensurate with the skills and qualifications required for specific roles to ensure the provision of quality services and the effective recruitment and retention of qualified, competent staff. (See *Compensation Guidelines for Early Childhood Professionals* [NAEYC 1993].)

- Decisions related to how programs are staffed and how children are grouped result in increased opportunities for children to experience continuity of relationships with teachers and other children. Such strategies include but are not limited to multiage grouping and multiyear teacher-child relationships (Katz, Evangelou, & Hartman 1990; Zero to Three 1995; Burke 1996).

3. Resources and expertise are available to provide safe, stimulating learning environments with a sufficient number and variety of appropriate materials and equipment for the age group served (Bronson 1995; Kendrick, Kaufmann, & Messenger 1995).

4. Adequate systems for regulating and monitoring the quality of early childhood programs are in place (see position on licensing [NAEYC 1987]; accreditation criteria and procedures [NAEYC 1991]).

5. Community resources are available and used to support the comprehensive needs of children and families (Kagan 1991; NASBE 1991; Kagan et al. 1995; NCSL 1995).

6. When individual children do not make expected learning progress, neither grade retention nor social promotion are used; instead, initiatives such as more focused time, individualized instruction, tutoring, or other individual strategies are used to accelerate children's learning (Shepard & Smith 1989; Ross et al. 1995).

7. Early childhood programs use multiple indicators of progress in all development domains to evaluate the effect of the program on children's development and learning and regularly report children's progress to parents. Group-administered, standardized, multiple-choice achievement tests are not used before third grade, preferably before fourth grade. When such tests are used to demonstrate public accountability, a sampling method is used (see Shepard 1994).

REFERENCES

Adams, G., & J. Sandfort. 1994. *First steps, promising futures: State prekindergarten initiatives in the early 1990s.* Washington, DC: Children's Defense Fund.

Alexander, K.L., & D.R. Entwisle. 1988. *Achievement in the first 2 years of school: Patterns and processes.* Monographs of the Society for Research in Child Development, vol. 53, no. 2, serial no. 218. Ann Arbor: University of Michigan.

Arnett, J. 1989. Caregivers in day-care centers: Does training matter? *Journal of Applied Developmental Psychology* 10 (4): 541–52.

Asher, S., S. Hymel, & P. Renshaw. 1984. Loneliness in children. *Child Development* 55: 1456–64.

Barnett, W.S. 1995. Long-term effects of early childhood programs on cognitive and school outcomes. *The Future of Children* 5 (3): 25–50.

Bergen, D. 1988. *Play as a medium for learning and development.* Portsmouth, NH: Heinemann.

Berk, L.E. 1996. *Infants and children: Prenatal through middle childhood.* 2d ed. Needham Heights, MA: Allyn & Bacon.

Berk, L., & A. Winsler. 1995. *Scaffolding children's learning: Vygotsky and early childhood education.* Washington, DC: NAEYC.

Berruetta-Clement, J.R., L.J. Schweinhart, W.S. Barnett, A.S. Epstein, & D.P. Weikart. 1984. *Changed lives: The effects of the Perry Preschool Program on youths through age 19.* Monographs of the High/Scope Educational Research Foundation, no. 8. Ypsilanti, MI: High/Scope Press.

Bodrova, E., & D. Leong. 1996. *Tools of the mind: The Vygotskian approach to early childhood education.* Englewood Cliffs, NJ: Merrill/ Prentice Hall.

Bowlby, J. 1969. *Attachment and loss: Vol. 1. Attachment.* New York: Basic.

Bowman, B. 1994. The challenge of diversity. *Phi Delta Kappan* 76 (3): 218–25.

Bowman, B., & F. Stott. 1994. Understanding development in a cultural context: The challenge for teachers. In *Diversity and developmentally appropriate practices: Challenges for early childhood education,* eds. B. Mallory & R. New, 119–34. New York: Teachers College Press.

Bredekamp, S., ed. 1987. *Developmentally appropriate practice in early childhood programs serving children from birth through age 8.* Exp. ed. Washington, DC: NAEYC.

Bredekamp, S. 1993a. Reflections on Reggio Emilia. *Young Children* 49 (1): 13–17.

Bredekamp, S. 1993b. The relationship between early childhood education and early childhood special education: Healthy marriage or family feud? *Topics in Early Childhood Special Education* 13 (3): 258–73.

Bredekamp, S., & T. Rosegrant, eds. 1992. *Reaching potentials: Appropriate curriculum and assessment for young children, volume 1.* Washington, DC: NAEYC.

Bredekamp, S., & T. Rosegrant, eds. 1995. *Reaching potentials: Transforming early childhood curriculum and assessment, volume 2.* Washington, DC: NAEYC.

Bronfenbrenner, U. 1979. *The ecology of human development: Experiments by nature and design.* Cambridge, MA: Harvard University Press.

Bronfenbrenner, U. 1989. Ecological systems theory. In *Annals of child development,* Vol. 6, ed. R. Vasta, 187–251. Greenwich, CT: JAI Press.

Bronfenbrenner, U. 1993. The ecology of cognitive development: Research models and fugitive findings. In *Development in context,* eds. R.H. Wozniak & K.W. Fischer, 3–44. Hillsdale, NJ: Erlbaum.

Bronson, M.B. 1995. *The right stuff for children birth to 8: Selecting play materials to support development.* Washington, DC: NAEYC.

Brophy, J. 1992. Probing the subtleties of subject matter teaching. *Educational Leadership* 49 (7): 4–8.

Bruner, J.S. 1983. *Child's talk: Learning to use language.* New York: Norton.

Bruner, J.S. 1996. *The culture of education.* Cambridge, MA: Harvard University Press.

Bryant, D.M., R. Clifford, & E.S. Peisner. 1991. Best practices for beginners: Developmental appropriateness in kindergarten. *American Educational Research Journal* 28 (4): 783–803.

Burchinal, M., J. Robert, L. Nabo, & D. Bryant. 1996. Quality of center child care and infant cognitive and language development. *Child Development* 67 (2): 606–20.

Burke, D. 1996. Multi-year teacher/student relationships are a long-overdue arrangement. *Phi Delta Kappan* 77 (5): 360–61.

Caine, R., & G. Caine. 1991. *Making connections: Teaching and the human brain.* New York: Addison-Wesley.

Campbell, F., & C. Ramey. 1995. Cognitive and school outcomes for high-risk African-American students at middle adolescence: Positive effects of early intervention. *American Educational Research Journal* 32 (4): 743–72.

Carnegie Task Force on Learning in the Primary Grades. 1996. *Years of promise: A comprehensive learning strategy for America's children.* New York: Carnegie Corporation of New York.

Carta, J., I. Schwartz, J. Atwater, & S. McConnell. 1991. Developmentally appropriate practice: Appraising its usefulness for young children with disabilities. *Topics in Early Childhood Special Education* 11 (1): 120.

Case, R., & Y. Okamoto. 1996. *The role of central conceptual structures in the development of children's thought.* Monographs of the Society of Research in Child Development, vol. 61, no. 2, serial no. 246. Chicago: University of Chicago Press.

Charlesworth, R., C.H. Hart, D.C. Burts, & M. DeWolf. 1993. The LSU studies: Building a research base for developmentally appropriate practice. In *Perspectives on developmentally appropriate practice,* vol. 5 of *Advances in early education and day care*, ed. S. Reifel, 3–28. Greenwich, CT: JAI Press.

Chugani, H., M.E. Phelps, & J.C. Mazziotta. 1987. Positron emission tomography study of human brain functional development. *Annals of Neurology* 22 (4): 495.

Cohen, N., & K. Modigliani. 1994. The family-to-family project: Developing family child care providers. In *The early childhood career lattice: Perspectives on professional development,* eds. J. Johnson & J.B. McCracken, 106–10. Washington, DC: NAEYC.

Copple, C., I.E. Sigel, & R. Saunders. 1984. *Educating the young thinker: Classroom strategies for cognitive growth.* Hillsdale, NJ: Erlbaum.

Cost, Quality, & Child Outcomes Study Team. 1995. *Cost, quality, and child outcomes in child care centers, public report.* 2d ed. Denver: Economics Department, University of Colorado at Denver.

Dana Alliance for Brain Initiatives. 1996. *Delivering results: A progress report on brain research.* Washington, DC: Author.

DEC/CEC (Division for Early Childhood of the Council for Exceptional Children). 1994. Position on inclusion. *Young Children* 49 (5): 78.

DEC (Division for Early Childhood) Task Force on Recommended Practices. 1993. *DEC recommended practices: Indicators of quality in programs for infants and young children with special needs and their families.* Reston, VA: Council for Exceptional Children.

DEC/CEC & NAEYC (Division for Early Childhood of the Council for Exceptional Children & the National Association for the Education of Young Children. 1993. *Understanding the ADA—The Americans with Disabilities Act: Information for early childhood programs.* Pittsburgh, PA, & Washington, DC: Authors.

DeVries, R., & W. Kohlberg. 1990. *Constructivist early education: Overview and comparison with other programs.* Washington, DC: NAEYC.

Dewey, J. 1916. *Democracy and education: An introduction to the philosophy of education.* New York: Macmillan.

Durkin, D. 1987. A classroom-observation study of reading instruction in kindergarten. *Early Childhood Research Quarterly* 2 (3): 275–300.

Durkin, D. 1990. Reading instruction in kindergarten: A look at some issues through the lens of new basal reader materials. *Early Children Research Quarterly* 5 (3): 299–316.

Dweck, C. 1986. Motivational processes affecting learning. *American Psychologist* 41: 1030–48.

Dyson, A.H., & C. Genishi. 1993. Visions of children as language users: Language and language education in early childhood. In *Handbook of research on the education of young children*, ed. B. Spodek, 122–36. New York: Macmillan.

Edwards, C.P., & L. Gandini. 1989. Teachers' expectations about the timing of developmental skills: A cross-cultural study. *Young Children* 44 (4): 15–19.

Edwards, C., L. Gandini, & G. Forman, eds. 1993. *The hundred languages of children: The Reggio Emilia approach to early childhood education.* Norwood, NJ: Ablex.

Erikson, E. 1963. *Childhood and society.* New York: Norton.

Feeney, S., & K. Kipnis. 1992. *Code of ethical conduct & statement of commitment.* Washington, DC: NAEYC.

Fein, G. 1981. Pretend play: An integrative review. *Child Development* 52: 1095–118.

Fein, G., & M. Rivkin, eds. 1986. *The young child at play: Reviews of research.* Washington, DC: NAEYC.

Fenson, L., P. Dale, J.S. Reznick, E. Bates, D. Thal, & S. Pethick. 1994. *Variability in early communicative development.* Monographs of the Society for Research in Child Development, vol. 59, no. 2, serial no. 242. Chicago: University of Chicago Press.

Fernald, A. 1992. Human maternal vocalizations to infants as biologically relevant signals: An evolutionary perspective. In *The adapted mind: Evolutionary psychology and the generation of culture*, eds. J.H. Barkow, L. Cosmides, & J. Tooby, 391–428. New York: Oxford University Press.

Fields, T., W. Masi, S. Goldstein, S. Perry, & S. Parl. 1988. Infant day care facilities preschool social behavior. *Early Childhood Research Quarterly* 3 (4): 341–59.

Forman, G. 1994. Different media, different languages. In *Reflections on the Reggio Emilia approach,* eds. L. Katz & B. Cesarone, 37–46. Urbana, IL: ERIC Clearinghouse on EECE.

Forman, E.A., N. Minick, & C.A. Stone. 1993. *Contexts for learning: Sociocultural dynamics in children's development.* New York: Oxford University Press.

Francis, P., & P. Self. 1982. Imitative responsiveness of young children in day care and home settings: The importance of the child to caregiver ratio. *Child Study Journal* 12: 119–26.

Frede, E. 1995. The role of program quality in producing early childhood program benefits. *The Future of Children*, 5 (3): 115–132.

Frede, E., & W.S. Barnett. 1992. Developmentally appropriate public school preschool: A study of implementation of the High/Scope curriculum and its effects on disadvantaged children's skills at first grade. *Early Childhood Research Quarterly* 7 (4): 483–99.

Fromberg, D. 1992. Play. In *The early childhood curriculum: A review of current research*, 2d ed., ed. C. Seefeldt, 35–74. New York: Teachers College Press.

Galinsky, E., C. Howes, S. Kontos, & M. Shinn. 1994. *The study of children in family child care and relative care: Highlights of findings.* New York: Families and Work Institute.

Gallahue, D. 1993. Motor development and movement skill acquisition in early childhood education. In *Handbook of research on the education of young children,* ed. B. Spodek, 24–41. New York: Macmillan.

Gallahue, D. 1995. Transforming physical education curriculum. In *Reaching potentials: Transforming early childhood curriculum and assessment, volume 2,* eds. S. Bredekamp & T. Rosegrant, 125–44. Washington, DC: NAEYC.

Garbarino, J., N. Dubrow, K. Kostelny, & C. Pardo. 1992. *Children in danger: Coping with the consequences of community violence.* San Francisco: Jossey-Bass.

Gardner, H. 1983. *Frames of mind: The theory of multiple intelligences.* New York: Basic.

Gardner, H. 1991. *The unschooled mind: How children think and how schools should teach.* New York: Basic.

Gelman, R., & R. Baillargeon. 1983. A review of some Piagetian concepts. In *Handbook of Child Psychology*, vol. 3, ed. P.H. Mussen, 167–230. New York: Wiley.

Gelman, R., & E. Meck. 1983. Preschoolers' counting: Principles before skill. *Cognition* 13: 343–59.

Hale-Benson, J. 1986. *Black children: Their roots, cultures, and learning styles.* Rev. ed. Baltimore: Johns Hopkins University Press.

Herron, R., & B. Sutton-Smith. 1971. *Child's play.* New York: Wiley.

Hiebert, E.H., & J.M. Papierz. 1990. The emergent literacy construct and kindergarten and readiness books of basal reading series. *Early childhood Research Quarterly* 5 (3): 317–34.

Hohmann, M., & D. Weikart. 1995. *Educating young children: Active learning practices for preschool and child care programs.* Ypsilanti, MI: High/Scope Educational Research Foundation.

Hollestelle, K. 1993. At the core: Entrepreneurial skills for family child care providers. In *The early childhood career lattice: Perspectives on professional development*, eds. J. Johnson & J.B. McCracken, 63–65. Washington, DC: NAEYC.

Howes, C. 1983. Caregiver behavior in center and family day care. *Journal of Applied Developmental Psychology* 4: 96–107.

Howes, C. 1988. Relations between early child care and schooling. *Developmental Psychology* 24 (1): 53–57.

Howes, C., D.A. Phillips, M. Whitebook. 1992. Thresholds of quality: Implications for the social development of children in center-based child care. *Child Development* 63 (2): 449–60.

Howes, C., E. Smith, & E. Galinsky. 1995. *The Florida child care quality improvement study.* New York: Families and Work Institute.

Kagan, S.L. 1991. *United we stand: Collaboration for child care and early educaion services.* New York: Teachers College Press.

Kagan, S., S. Goffin, S. Golub, & E. Pritchard. 1995. *Toward systematic reform: Service integration for young children and their families.* Falls Church, VA: National Center for Service Integration.

Kamii, C., & J.K. Ewing. 1996. Basing teaching on Piaget's constructivism. *Childhood Education* 72 (5): 260–64.

Katz, L. 1995. *Talks with teachers of young children: A collection.* Norwood, NJ: Ablex.

Katz, L., & S. Chard. 1989. *Engaging children minds: The project approach.* Norwood, NJ: Ablex.

Katz, L., D. Evangelou, & J. Hartman. 1990. *The case for mixed-age grouping in early education.* Washington, DC: NAEYC.

Kendrick, A., R. Kaufmann, & K. Messenger, eds. 1995. *Healthy young children: A manual for programs.* Washington, DC: NAEYC.

Kohn, A. 1993. *Punished by rewards.* Boston: Houghton Mifflin.

Kostelnik, M., A. Soderman, & A. Whiren. 1993. *Developmentally appropriate programs in early childhood education.* New York: Macmillan.

Kuhl, P. 1994. Learning and representation in speech and language. *Current Opinion in Neurobiology* 4: 812–22.

Lary, R.T. 1990. Successful students. *Education Issues* 3 (2): 11–17.

Layzer, J.I., B.D. Goodson, & M. Moss. 1993. *Life in preschool: Volume one of an observational study of early childhood programs for disadvantaged four-year-olds.* Cambridge, MA: Abt Association.

Lazar, I., & R. Darlington. 1982. *Lasting effects of early education: A report from the consortium for longitudinal studies.* Monographs of the Society for Research in Child Development, vol. 47, nos. 2–3, serial no. 195. Chicago: University of Chicago Press.

Lee, V.E., J. Brooks-Gunn, & E. Schuur. 1988. Does Head Start work? A 1-year follow-up comparison of disadvantaged children attending Head Start, no preschool, and other preschool programs. *Developmental Psychology* 24 (2): 210–22.

Legters, N., & R.E. Slavin. 1992. Elementary students at risk: A status report. Paper commissioned by the Carnegie Corporation of New York for meeting on elementary-school reform. 12 June.

Levy, A.K., L. Schaefer, & P.C. Phelps. 1986. Increasing preschool effectiveness: Enhancing the language abilities of 3- and 4-year-old children through planned sociodramatic play. *Early Childhood Research Quarterly* 1 (2): 133–40.

Levy, A.K., C.H. Wolfgang, & M.A. Koorland. 1992. Sociodramatic play as a method for enhancing the language performance of kindergarten age students. *Early Childhood Research Quarterly* 7 (2): 245–62.

Malaguzzi, L. 1993. History, ideas, and basic philosophy. In *The hundred languages of children: The Reggio Emilia approach to early childhood education*, eds. C. Edwards, L. Gandini, & G. Forman, 41–89. Norwood, NJ: Ablex.

Mallory, B. 1992. Is it always appropriate to be developmental? Convergent models for early intervention practice. *Topics in Early Childhood Special Education* 11 (4): 1–12.

Mallory, B. 1994. Inclusive policy, practice, and theory for young children with developmental differences. In *Diversity and developmentally appropriate practices: Challenges for early childhood education*, eds. B. Mallory & R. New, 44–61. New York: Teachers College Press.

Mallory, B.L., & R.S. New. 1994a. *Diversity and developmentally appropriate practices: Challenges for early childhood education.* New York: Teachers College Press.

Mallory, B.L., & R.S. New. 1994b. Social constructivist theory and principles of inclusion: Challenges for early childhood special education. *Journal of Special Education* 28 (3): 322–37.

Marcon, R.A. 1992. Differential effects of three preschool models on inner-city 4-year-olds. *Early Childhood Research Quarterly* 7 (4): 517–30.

Maslow, A. 1954. *Motivation and personality.* New York: Harper & Row.

Miller, L.B., & R.P. Bizzell. 1984. Long-term effects of four preschool programs: Ninth and tenth-grade results. *Child Development* 55 (4): 1570–87.

Mitchell, A., M. Seligson, & F. Marx. 1989. *Early childhood programs and the public schools.* Dover, MA: Auburn House.

Morrow, L.M. 1990. Preparing the classroom environment to promote literacy during play. *Early Childhood Research Quarterly* 5 (4): 537–54.

NAEYC. 1987. *NAEYC position statement on licensing and other forms of regulation of early childhood programs in centers and family day care.* Washington, DC: Author.

NAEYC. 1991. *Accreditation criteria and procedures of the National Academy of Early Childhood Programs.* Rev. ed. Washington, DC: Author.

NAEYC. 1993. *Compensation guidelines for early childhood professionals.* Washington, DC: Author.

NAEYC. 1994. NAEYC position statement: A conceptual framework for early childhood professional development, adopted November 1993. *Young Children* 49 (3): 68–77.

NAEYC. 1996a. NAEYC position statement: Responding to linguistic and cultural diversity—Recommendations for effective early childhood education. *Young Children* 51 (2): 412.

NAEYC. 1996b. NAEYC position statement: Technology and young children—Ages three through eight. *Young Children* 51 (6): 11–16.

NAEYC & NAECS/SDE (National Association of Early Childhood Specialists in State Departments of Education). 1992. Guidelines for appropriate curriculum content and assessment in programs serving children ages 3 through 8. In *Reaching potentials: Appropriate curriculum and assessment for young children, volume 1*, eds. S. Bredekamp & T. Rosegrant, 9–27. Washington, DC: NAEYC.

NASBE (National Association of State Boards of Education). 1991. *Caring communities: Supporting young children and families*. Alexandria, VA: Author.

Natriello, G., E. McDill, & A. Pallas. 1990. *Schooling disadvantaged children: Racing against catastrophe*. New York: Teachers College Press.

NCES (National Center for Education Statistics). 1993. *The condition of education, 1993*. Washington, DC: U.S. Department of Education.

NCSL (National Conference of State Legislatures). 1995. *Early childhood care and education: An investment that works*. Denver: Author.

NEGP (National Education Goals Panel). 1991. *National education goals report: Building a nation of learners*. Washington, DC: Author.

New, R. 1993. Cultural variations on developmentally appropriate practice: Challenges to theory and practice. In *The hundred languages of children: The Reggio Emilia approach to early childhood education*, eds. C. Edwards, L. Gandini, & G. Forman, 215–32. Norwood, NJ: Ablex.

New, R. 1994. Culture, child development, and developmentally appropriate practices: Teachers as collaborative researchers. In *Diversity and developmentally appropriate practices: Challenges for early childhood education*, eds. B. Mallory & R. New, 65–83. New York: Teachers College Press.

Nye, B.A., J. Boyd-Zaharias, & B.D. Fulton. 1994. *The lasting benefits study: A continuing analysis of the effect of small class size in kindergarten through third grade on student achievement test scores in subsequent grade levels seventh grade (1992–93), technical report*. Nashville: Center of Excellence for Research in Basic Skills, Tennessee State University.

Nye, B.A., J. Boyd-Zaharias, B.D. Fulton, & M.P. Wallenhorst. 1992. Smaller classes really are better. *The American School Board Journal* 179 (5): 31–33.

Parker, J.G., & S.R. Asher. 1987. Peer relations and later personal adjustment: Are low-accepted children at risk? *Psychology Bulletin* 102 (3): 357–89.

Phillips, C.B. 1994. The movement of African-American children through sociocultural contexts: A case of conflict resolution. In *Diversity and developmentally appropriate practices: Challenges for early childhood education*, eds. B. Mallory & R. New, 137–54. New York: Teachers College Press.

Phillips, D.A., K. McCartney, & S. Scarr. 1987. Child care quality and children's social development. *Developmental Psychology* 23 (4): 537–43.

Piaget, J. 1952. *The origins of intelligence in children*. New York: International Universities Press.

Plomin, R. 1994a. *Genetics and experience: The interplay between nature and nurture*. Thousand Oaks, CA: Sage.

Plomin, R. 1994b. Nature, nurture, and social development. *Social Development* 3: 37–53.

Powell, D. 1994. Parents, pluralism, and the NAEYC statement on developmentally appropriate practice. In *Diversity and developmentally appropriate practices: Challenges for early childhood education*, eds. B. Mallory & R. New, 166–82. New York: Teachers College Press.

Pramling, I. 1991. Learning about "the shop": An approach to learning in preschool. *Early Children Research Quarterly* 6 (2): 151–66.

Resnick, L. 1996. Schooling and the workplace: What relationship? In *Preparing youth for the 21st century,* 21–27. Washington, DC: Aspen Institute.

Rogoff, B. 1990. *Apprenticeship in thinking: Cognitive development in social context*. New York: Oxford University Press.

Rogoff, B., J. Mistry, A. Goncu, & C. Mosier. 1993. *Guided participation in cultural activity by toddlers and caregivers*. Monographs of the Society for Research in Child Development, vol. 58, no. 8, serial no. 236. Chicago: University of Chicago Press.

Ross, S.M., L.J. Smith, J. Casey, & R.E. Slavin. 1995. Increasing the academic success of disadvantaged children: An examination of alternative early intervention programs. *American Educational Research Journal* 32 (4): 773–800.

Ruopp, R., J. Travers, F. Glantz, & C. Coelen. 1979. *Children at the center: Final report of the National Day Care Study*. Cambridge, MA: ABT Associates.

Sameroff, A., & S. McDonough. 1994. Educational implications of developmental transitions: Revisiting the 5- to 7-year shift. *Phi Delta Kappan* 76 (3): 188–93.

Scarr, S., & K. McCartney. 1983. How people make their own environments: A theory of genotype—environment effects. *Child Development* 54: 425–35.

Schrader, C.T. 1989. Written language use within the context of young children's symbolic play. *Early Childhood Research Quarterly* 4 (2): 225–44.

Schrader, C.T. 1990. Symbolic play as a curricular tool for early literacy development. *Early Childhood Research Quarterly* 5 (1): 79–103.

Schweinhart, L.J., & D.P. Weikart. 1996. *Lasting differences: The High/Scope preschool curriculum comparison study through age 23.* Monographs of the High/Scope Educational Research Foundation, no 12. Ypsilanti, MI: High/Scope Press.

Schweinhart, L.J., H.V. Barnes, & D.P. Weikart. 1993. *Significant benefits: The High/Scope Perry Preschool Study through age 27.* Monographs of the High/Scope Educational Research Foundation, no. 10, Ypsilanti, MI: High/Scope Press.

Schweinhart, L.J., D.P. Weikart, & M.B. Larner. 1986. Child-initiated activities in early childhood programs may help prevent delinquency. *Early Childhood Research Quarterly* 1 (3): 303–12.

Seefeldt, C., ed. 1992. *The early childhood curriculum: A review of current research.* 2d ed. New York: Teachers College Press.

Seifert, K. 1993. Cognitive development and early childhood education. In *Handbook of research on the education of young children,* ed. B. Spodek, 923. New York: Macmillan.

Seppanen, P.S., D. Kaplan deVries, & M. Seligson. 1993. *National study of before and after school programs.* Portsmouth, NH: RMC Research Corp.

Shepard, L. 1994. The challenges of assessing young children appropriately. *Phi Delta Kappan* 76 (3): 206–13.

Shepard, L.A., & M.L. Smith. 1988. Escalating academic demand in kindergarten: Some nonsolutions. *Elementary School Journal* 89 (2): 135–46.

Shepard, L.A., & M.L. Smith. 1989. *Flunking grades: Research and policies on retention.* Bristol, PA: Taylor & Francis.

Slavin, R., N. Karweit, & N. Madden, eds. 1989. *Effective programs for students at-risk.* Boston: Allyn & Bacon.

Smilansky, S., & L. Shefatya. 1990. *Facilitating play: A medium for promoting cognitive, socioemotional, and academic development in young children.* Gaithersburg, MD: Psychosocial & Educational Publications.

Spodek, B., ed. 1993. *Handbook of research on the education of young children.* New York: Macmillan.

Sroufe, L.A., R.G. Cooper, & G.B. DeHart. 1992. *Child development: Its nature and course.* 2d ed. New York: Knopf.

Stern, D. 1985. *The psychological world of the human infant.* New York: Basic.

Stremmel, A.J., & V.R. Fu. 1993. Teaching in the zone of proximal development: Implications for responsive teaching practice. *Child and Youth Care Forum* 22 (5): 337–50.

Taylor, J.M., & W.S. Taylor. 1989. *Communicable diseases and young children in group settings*. Boston: Little, Brown. Tobin, J., D. Wu, & D. Davidson. 1989. *Preschool in three cultures*. New Haven, CT: Yale University Press.

U.S. Department of Health & Human Services. 1996. *Head Start performance standards*. Washington, DC: Author.

Vandell, D.L., & M.A. Corasanti. 1990. Variations in early child care: Do they predict subsequent social, emotional, and cognitive differences? *Early Childhood Research Quarterly* 5 (4): 555–72.

Vandell, D.L., & C.D. Powers. 1983. Day care quality and children's freeplay activities. *American Journal of Orthopsychiatry* 53 (4): 493–500.

Vandell, D.L., V.K. Henderson, & K.S. Wilson. 1988. A longitudinal study of children with day-care experiences of varying quality. *Child Development* 59 (5): 1286–92.

Vygotsky, L. 1978. *Mind in society: The development of higher psychological processes*. Cambridge, MA: Harvard University Press.

Wardle, F. 1996. Proposal: An anti-bias and ecological model for multicultural education. *Childhood Education* 72 (3): 152–56.

Wertsch, J. 1985. *Culture, communication, and cognition: Vygotskian perspectives*. New York: Cambridge University Press.

White, S.H. 1965. Evidence for a hierarchical arrangement of learning processes. In *Advances in child development and behavior,* eds. L.P. Lipsitt & C.C. Spiker, 187–220. New York: Academic Press.

Whitebook, M., C. Howes, & D. Phillips. 1989. *The national child care staffing study: Who cares? Child care teachers and the quality of care in America*. Final report. Oakland, CA: Child Care Employee Project.

Wieder, S., & S.I. Greenspan. 1993. The emotional basis of learning. In *Handbook of research on the education of young children,* ed. B. Spodek, 77–104. New York: Macmillan.

Willer, B. 1990. *Reaching the full cost of quality in early childhood programs*. Washington, DC: NAEYC.

Willer, B., S.L. Hofferth, E.E. Kisker, P. Divine-Hawkins, E. Farquhar, & F.B. Glantz. 1991. *The demand and supply of child care in 1990*. Washington, DC: NAEYC.

Witkin, H. 1962. *Psychological differentiation: Studies of development*. New York: Wiley.

Wolery, M., & J. Wilbers, eds. 1994. *Including children with special needs in early childhood programs*. Washington, DC: NAEYC.

Wolery, M., P. Strain, & D. Bailey. 1992. Reaching potentials of children with special needs. In *Reaching Potentials: Appropriate curriculum and assessment for young children, volume 1,* eds. S. Bredekamp & T. Rosegrant, 92–111. Washington, DC: NAEYC.

Zero to Three: The National Center. 1995. *Caring for infants and toddlers in groups: Developmentally appropriate practice*. Arlington, VA: Author.

GUIDELINES FOR DEVELOPMENTALLY APPROPRIATE PRACTICE

NAEYC's DAP guidelines can be implemented in your daily work with children:

- Create a caring environment among children and adults

  Children:

  - learn personal responsibility

  - develop constructive relationships with others

  - respect individual and cultural differences

  Adults:

  - get to know each child, taking into account individual differences and developmental level

  - adjust the pace and content of the curriculum so that children can be successful most of the time

  - bring each child's culture and language into the setting

  - expect children to be tolerant of others' differences

- Allow children to select and initiate their own activities

  Children:

  - learn through active involvement in a variety of learning experiences

  - build independence by taking on increasing responsibilities

  - initiate their own activities to follow their interests

  Adults:

  - provide a variety of materials and activities that are concrete and real

  - provide a variety of work places and spaces

  - arrange the environment so that children can work alone or in groups

  - extend children's learning by posing problems, asking thought-provoking questions

- add complexity to tasks as needed

- model, demonstrate, and provide information so children can progress in their learning

- Enable children to develop a deeper understanding of key concepts and skills

Children:

- engage in activities that reflect their current interests

- plan and predict outcomes of their research

- share information and knowledge with others

Adults:

- plan related activities and experiences that broaden children's knowledge and skills

- design the curriculum to foster important skills like literacy and numeracy

- adapt instruction for children who are ahead or behind the age-appropriate expectations

- plan the curriculum so that children achieve important developmental goals

- Help children develop a positive self-image within a democratic community

Children:

- learn through reading books about other cultures

- read about current events and discuss how these relate to different cultures

- accept differences among their peers, including children with disabilities

Adults:

- provide culturally-relevant and non-sexist activities and materials that foster children's self-identity

- design the learning environment so that children can learn new skills while using their native language

- allow children to demonstrate their learning using their own language

- Develop children's awareness of the importance of community involvement

Children:

- are ready and eager to learn about the world outside their immediate environment

- are open to considering different ways of thinking or doing things

- can benefit from contact with others outside their homes or child care setting

Adults:

- encourage awareness of the community at large

- plan experiences in facilities within the community

- bring outside resources and volunteers into the child care setting

- encourage children to plan their involvement based on their own interests

PROFESSIONAL ORGANIZATIONS

When looking to further your career development, a professional organization is a great place to start. There are several organizations, some of which have state or local affiliates:

Association for Education International (ACEI)
The Olney Professional Building
17904 Georgia Avenue, Suite 215
Olney, MD 20832
Phone: 800-423-2563 or 301-570-2122
Fax: 301-570-2212
Website: http://www.acei.org

ACEI is an international organization dedicated to promoting the best educational practices throughout the world.

Specific membership benefits:

- Workshops and travel/study tours abroad
- Four issues per year of the journals *Childhood Education* and the *Journal of Research in Childhood Education*
- Hundreds of resources for parents and teachers, including books, pamphlets, audiotapes, and videotapes

National After School Association (NAA)
1137 Washington Street
Boston, MA 02124
Phone: 617-298-5012
Fax: 617-298-5022
Website: http://www.naaweb.org

NAA is a national organization dedicated to providing information, technical assistance, and resources concerning children in out-of-school programs. Members include teachers, policy makers, and administrators representing all public, private, and community-based sectors of after-school programs.

Specific member benefits:

- A subscription to the NAA journal, *School-Age Review*
- A companion membership in state affiliates
- Discounts on NAA publications and products
- Discount on NAA annual conference registration
- Opportunity to be an NAA accreditation endorser
- Public policy representatives in Washington, DC

National Association for the Education of Young Children (NAEYC)
1509 16th Street, NW
Washington DC 20036
800-424-2460
www.naeyc.org
Email membership@naeyc.org

NAEYC is a national lobbying organization for legislature that affects children and families.

Specific membership benefits:
Comprehensive Members receive all the benefits of regular membership described below, plus annually receive five or six books immediately after their release by NAEYC.

Regular and student members receive:

- Six issues of *Young Children*, which includes timely articles on pertinent issues, as well as suggestions and strategies for enhancing children's learning
- Reduced registration fees at NAEYC-sponsored local and national conferences and seminars
- Discounted prices on hundreds of books, videos, brochures, and posters from NAEYC's extensive catalog of materials
- Access to the *Members Only* website, including links to additional resources and chat sites for communication with other professionals

National Association of Child Care Professionals (NACCP)
P.O. Box 90723
Austin, TX 78709
800-537-1118
www.naccp.org

Specific membership benefits:

Management Tools of the Trade™

"Your membership provides complete and FREE access (a $79 value) to these effective management tools that provide technical assistance in human resource management. In addition, members will receive NACCP's quarterly trade journals **(Professional Connections©, Teamwork©, and Caring for Your Children©)** to help you stay on top of hot issues in child care. Each edition also includes a Tool of the Trade™."

National Child Care Association (NCCA)
1016 Rosser St.
Conyers GA 30012
800-543-7161
www.nccanet.org

NCCA is a national association for licensed child care providers. It offers business tips, money management tools and professional development opportunities.

Specific membership benefits:

- As the only recognized voice in Washington DC, NCCA has great influence on our legislators
- Professional development opportunities are available

OTHER ORGANIZATIONS TO CONTACT:.

Council for Exceptional Children
1110N. Glebe Road, Suite 300,
Arlington, VA 22201
888-CEC-SPED
www.cec.sped.org
Journal: *CEC Today*

International Reading Association
800 Barksdale Road
P.O. Box 8139
Newark, DE 19714
800-336-READ
www.reading.org
Journal: *The Reading Teacher*

International Society for the Prevention of Child Abuse and Neglect
25 W. 560 Geneva Road, suite L2C
Carol Stream, IL 60188
630-221-1311
www.ipscan.org
Journal: *Child Abuse and Neglect: The International Journal*

National Association for Bilingual Education
Union Center Plaza
810 First Street, NE
Washington DC 20002
www.nabe.org
Journal: *NABE Journal of Research and Practice*

National Association for Family Child Care
P.O. Box 10373
Des Moines, IA 50306
800-359-3817
www.nafcc.org
Journal: *The National Perspective*

National Black Child Development Institute
1023 15th Ave. NW
Washington DC 20002
202-833-2220
www.nbcdi.org

National Education Organization (NEA)
1201 16th St. NW
Washington, DC 20036
202-833-4000
www.nea.org
Journals: *Works4Me and NEA Focus* (online subscription)

National Head Start Association
1651 Prince Street
Alexandria VA 22314
703-739-0875
www.nhsa.org
Journal: *Children and Families*

The Children's Defense Fund
25 E. St. NW
Washington DC 20001
202-628-8787
www.childrensdefense.org

Zero to Three: National Center for Infants, Toddlers, and Families
2000M. Street NW, Suite 200
Washington DC 20036
202-638-1144
www.zerotothree.org
Journal: *Zero to Three*

CASE STUDIES

These are a few brief scenarios and possible solutions to problems you may encounter in your classroom:

A child with Autism will be starting in your classroom on Monday. You have heard that the child throws tantrums and does not speak.

What would your response be?

Possible solutions:

- Ask for any behavior contracts from past school settings
- Ask for permission to talk to the parent about what strategies work at home
- Find out what the child likes to play with and what rewards interest the child
- Prepare the other children for a new student who needs help learning to talk and suggest what the children might do to encourage communication

A child who is deaf will be joining your class in two weeks. You do not know any sign language.

What would your response be?

Possible solutions:

- Pick up a sign language book at the local library
- Look up finger spelling on the Internet
- Learn basic signs for hello, good bye, bathroom, eat, stop, love, and the child's name
- Teach the children in your class to use those signs as well

A new wheelchair ramp is going in at your facility, and the children are curious as to why.

What would your response be?

Possible solutions:

- You tell the children that some people have legs that do not always work the way they are supposed to and that the ramp will help them enter the building so they can play with the children.

- We want everyone to be able to see our wonderful school, so we are making it open to everyone.

C

ISSUES AND TRENDS

Children with exceptionalities are unique individuals who want their needs met as any other person would. They want to be recognized as individuals who are the exception to the rule and not the different one. To fascilitate these goals, the law has been updated to include what is called "people first" language: when referring to a person who is different, you must say, "child with autism" or "person with . . ." and list the exceptionality. It is a different way of looking at things, but it makes sense. I know that I want to be known as Jennifer and not always as Meaghan, Katelyn and Christopher's mom or David's wife. I am a person, too.

Another trend that we see is the ongoing movement toward inclusion. Inclusion is the old mainstreaming and involves including a child with exceptionalities in every aspect of life as a normally developing child would be included. More than merely including them in music, art, library, computers, and physical education, inclusion places them in classrooms with normally developing peers. The teacher is given support through a special education partner or consultant to best meet the needs of the child in every day classroom experiences. Instead of separation, we now have inclusion.

No Child Left Behind also addresses the children with exceptionalities and how they can not be left behind their normally developing peers. Schools have to find a way to bring these children as close to the third grade level as they are capable. The teacher can no longer fall on the excuse, "well they have special needs." The teacher is challenged to find ways to open doors and not close them, so that these children will not be left behind. The technology part of the law further helps these children to succeed and to be a part of the regular classroom. It requires schools to allow children access to technology and require it as part of the curriculum.